PRAISE FOR *TO THE MARTYRS*

Yes, sometimes "silence is golden," but not when it comes to the widespread vicious persecution of our brother and sister Christians around the world. It's time to shout in defense of these innocent people who are tempted to wonder why their co-religionists around the world—us!—are so quiet. Thanks, Cardinal Wuerl, for leading the shout!

—His Eminence Cardinal Timothy M. Dolan
Archbishop of New York

Cardinal Wuerl's eloquent historical survey of Christian martyrdom is very appropriate, especially during these days of increased persecution of men, women, and children who embrace Jesus Christ as their Lord and Savior. As the Lord Jesus Christ said, "If they persecuted me they will persecute you." This is because Christians are called to live according to compassion, mercy, and love in a world that often rejects the message of the Gospel with violence and persecution.

—Most Rev. Demetrios of America
Archbishop of the Greek Orthodox Archdiocese of America

Cardinal Donald Wuerl shines a bright light on the harsh truth that more Christians are dying today for their belief in Jesus Christ than at any other time in history. He provides a compelling historical perspective, applying lessons of the past that move the reader to a greater solidarity with and for the martyrs of today, both for the sake of the survival of the most ancient Christian communities and for the sake of our own humanity.

—Most Rev. David A. Zubik
Bishop of Pittsburgh

The book is a brief and yet telling account of the Christian martyrs and can be a great source of inspiration and strength for all those who are undergoing persecution of various types in our modern times. The author, in genuine solidarity with all who suffer for the sake of Christ and the Gospel, extends an invitation to break our silence and to act on behalf of the modern day martyrs. This is a very valuable and timely tribute to Christian martyrdom.

—Most Rev. Thomas Mar Eusebius
Bishop of the Syro-Malankara Catholic Apostolic Exarchate in the United States

This smart, impassioned, and incisive book is like an alarm bell in the night, waking the world to the awful truth of the martyrdom of Christians happening today all over the world. It provides Christians and non-Christians alike a wonderful primer in the spirituality of the martyrs. Anyone interested in the future of the Church and in the enduring power of Christian witness ought to read it.

—Most Rev. Robert Barron
Auxiliary Bishop of the Archdiocese of Los Angeles

A fascinating and important book, bringing up front to our consciousness the sacrifices made by so many thousands to preserve our Catholic Christian faith. Faced with similar and escalating threats today, dare we fail to make the same sacrifice?

—Marcus Grodi
Founder and President,
The Coming Home Network International

Cardinal Wuerl's *To the Martyrs* is not only highly informative but deeply moving—a historical survey and a theological reflection as timely and urgent as today's news. Hardly the least significant factor in the rising tide of religious persecution in many parts of the world—including even the United States—is the indifference and complacency of government officials, journalists, and, sad to say, entirely too many of the victims' fellow Christians. Read *To the Martyrs*, learn from it, and join the fight to protect religious liberty.

—Russell Shaw
Veteran journalist, author of American Church

Cardinal Wuerl has penned a powerful and positive book! The Church grows from the seed of the blood of the martyrs. The Cardinal has raised the clarion call that the era of martyrdom is not only in the distant past but upon us once more. As in times past we will rise from the ashes and grow stronger than ever before. It is a time to raise our voices! This book is an energetic encouragement in Christ and the Church!

—John Michael Talbot
Founder, Spiritual Father, and General Minister,
The Brothers and Sisters of Charity

The silence of Western Christians—and even Christian leaders—in the face of acts of persecution and genocide being committed against their fellow believers elsewhere in the world is a scandal. Yet the voices of a noble few have been raised—none more forcefully and consistently than that of Cardinal Donald Wuerl. In his powerful book, *To the Martyrs: A Reflection on the Supreme Christian Witness*, Cardinal Wuerl challenges us to stand in solidarity with the victims and add our voices to his.

—Robert P. George
McCormick Professor of Jurisprudence, Princeton University

When one Christian is persecuted, all Christians are persecuted. Elie Wiesel warned us: "To remain silent and indifferent is the greatest sin of all." Read this book, talk about this book, then write to your congressmen and senators. It is time that we took action on behalf of persecuted Christians.

—Matthew Kelly
Author of Rediscover Jesus *and*
Founder of the Dynamic Catholic Institute

In his book, *To the Martyrs: A Reflection on the Supreme Christian Witness,* Cardinal Wuerl once again sounds the alarm and reminds us of the daily—yes daily, and yes, in our day—martyrdom of Christians. Cardinal Wuerl pulls back the curtain on this tragic drama, which is played out in far too many countries in the world: Iraq, Syria, China, North Korea, Sudan, Pakistan just to mention a few. Religious freedom is a God-given right, but is often taken away by so many enemies of truth. Cardinal Wuerl, thank you for once again sounding the alarm.

—Most Rev. Gregory John Mansour
Bishop of the Eparchy of Saint Maron of Brookyln

Cardinal Wuerl has produced not only a comprehensive account of what it has meant to be a martyr in the past, he has warned us about the forces that contribute to Christian persecution even today—and threaten worse in the future. We should all take his conclusion very much to heart: Christians must always be prepared to be faithful to the very end.

—Robert Royal
Author of The Catholic Martyrs of the Twentieth Century
President, Faith and Reason Institute

In this compelling book Cardinal Donald Wuerl brings urgent attention to the suffering and martyrdom of Christians occurring today in nations around the world. He gives voice to the voiceless by telling their stories of suffering and death. As you read this informative call to action, keep in mind the maxim, "One who remains silent, consents." The author strives to ensure that future generations will not be able to say of this generation that they were complicit by silence in something as horrendous as the religious cleansing of nations.

—Most Rev. Stefan Soroka
Archbishop of the Ukrainian Catholic Archeparchy
of Philadelphia Metropolitan of Ukrainian Catholics
in the United States

Ours is an age of Christian martyrs! Yet the world knows them not and little venerates their passing. This book is a trumpet call for all Christians to rise up on behalf of their persecuted brothers and sisters. Their suffering must stop; their violent deaths must end; their lives must be saved! Cardinal Wuerl has heard their cry and so must the world.

—Fr. Thomas G. Weinandy, O.F.M., Cap.
Dominican House of Studies, Washington DC,
Member of the International Theological Commission

TO THE
MARTYRS

A Reflection on the Supreme Christian Witness

TO THE
MARTYRS

A Reflection on the Supreme Christian Witness

CARDINAL DONALD WUERL
ARCHBISHOP OF WASHINGTON, D.C.

EMMAUS
ROAD
PUBLISHING
Steubenville, Ohio

EMMAUS
ROAD
PUBLISHING

1468 Parkview Circle
Steubenville, Ohio 43952

© 2015 Donald W. Wuerl
All rights reserved. Published 2015
Printed in the United States of America
Library of Congress Control Number: 2015950545
ISBN: 978-1-941447-39-0

Cover design and layout by Mairead Cameron

Dedicated to the honor of those Christians who are suffering for the Faith today. They are many.

Table of Contents

Foreword

Today, martyrdom is often thought of in terms of a Christian's *murder* instead of a Christian's *witness*. And yet, as Cardinal Wuerl points out, the very word "martyr" means "witness"—and there can be no greater witness than giving up one's life for the Faith. As Christians, we are all called to be *witnesses*, and *witnesses* do not change their mission or message even if, like Christ, they face death.

Among the many expressions of Christian witness, martyrdom has a number of unique traits. It entails fidelity to Christ on the part of the Christian and lethal hatred of Christ on the part of the killer. There is no litmus test of knowledge or even explicit willingness to become a martyr.

Certainly, many go willingly to the scaffold and refuse to renounce their faith when offered the choice of apostatizing or losing their lives. Such martyrs—from the early Church on—fill our martyrology. Others know that the Christian life challenges the norms of the powerful and yet the Christian does not conform. One thinks of two of the great martyrs for marriage, St. Thomas More and St. John Fisher, killed for not condoning King Henry VIII's divorce and remarriage, and his subsequent attempt to subordinate the Church to himself. In more recent years, we have examples like Blessed Peter To

Rot, killed in the Japanese occupation of Papua New Guinea in 1945, whose death St. John Paul II described when beatifying him on January 17, 1995:

> When the authorities legalized and encouraged polygamy, Blessed Peter knew it to be against Christian principles and firmly denounced this practice. Because the Spirit of God dwelt in him, he fearlessly proclaimed *the truth about the sanctity of marriage.* He refused to take the "easy way" of moral compromise. "I have to fulfill *my duty as a Church witness to Jesus Christ,*" he explained.

But others suffer martyrdom without choice. They receive no moment to decide to persist in their faith; some are unaware of what is about to befall them; and others may lack a mature understanding of the Faith. Numerous children, for example, have suffered martyrdom for the simple fact that they are Christians, while others lose their lives *en masse* in church bombings or targeted killings.

Whatever the circumstances of martyrdom, these examples should elicit two reactions from us: to marvel at the strength of those who suffer and to have a realization that, in a profound way, being a Christian martyr is not simply holding on to God but being held by Him.

In every martyrdom is a kind of passionate embrace between God and martyr. A love that refuses to be broken even by cruelty and death.

As the Song of Songs says, "love is strong as death" (8:6). And as the martyr knows, such a death brings the promise of eternal life.

While most Christians do not experience the threat of serious repercussions for practicing their faith, there are millions of Christians in some parts of the world who live each day in fear. They are silenced from speaking about their faith. They worship knowing that every Mass could be their last. They suffer penalties, mockery, or even violent persecution because they believe in the One who taught them to love one another. In the world of many Christians, confessing their faith is a dangerous way to live.

Like Cardinal Wuerl, I too have had the honor over the years to speak with survivors of persecution. Many live in or have fled the lands where the generic fear of war has given way to violence directed explicitly against Christians. Listening to their testimonies about what they and others have suffered moves me without fail. The witness they provide is not only for themselves but certainly is also for their descendants and, indeed, for all of us.

In many ways, these witnesses to Christ—both those martyred and their suffering brethren—can truly be called "People of the Beatitudes," for they powerfully embody so much of Christ's great Sermon on the Mount in their lives. They are poor in spirit; they and their families mourn; they hunger and thirst for righteousness; they are peacemakers; and above all, they are persecuted for the sake of righteousness (Matthew 5:3–12). Because of Christ, they are insulted, persecuted, and evil is spoken of them. And it is these virtues and experience, all born for the love of Christ, that make them truly, in Christ's words, "Blessed."

Today, many of these Christians live in the Middle East. Theirs is the land of another martyr, the Apostle Thomas. His skepticism of our Lord's Resurrection earned him the nickname "Doubting Thomas." But the Risen Christ appeared to him so that he might believe, and St. Thomas became a great missionary. Within a few centuries, the Faith spread as far as India, and millions were baptized.

When Christ appeared to Thomas after the Resurrection, the Lord declared, "Blessed are those who have not seen and have believed" (John 20:29).

Martyrs also inherit this title of "Blessed" when they choose a future based on faith rather than a life they have already "seen."

Today, Christians around the world are being called to consider the lives and deaths of other martyrs whose witness should not be lost on us. Rather, their witness must motivate us to take our faith more seriously. We must cheerfully endure whatever suffering is required of us to defend the Faith—and look to the example of the martyrs for inspiration.

So let your heart be deeply moved as you read these pages. In every chapter a cloud of witnesses speaks of unconditional love and the desire to love Him with one's whole heart and whole life. In this work, Cardinal Wuerl exercises an admirable form of pastoral care that brings together a depth of insight and a richness of historical witness to educate and inspire. I hope it will encourage you, as it did me, to appreciate even more deeply our faith and the immense generosity of God in giving women and men courage and strength and, yes, even joy in the face of persecution. For the joy of being loved by Him surpasses all else. Let us listen to these witnesses, and perhaps the strength of our belief may increase and we, too, might be called "Blessed."

—Carl A. Anderson
Supreme Knight
Knights of Columbus

Preface

In many societies today, the utterance of a simple phrase, "I am a Christian," is a crime punishable by death. So widespread is this persecution that Pope Francis called it a "third world war, waged piecemeal . . . a form of genocide."[1]

The Holy Father spoke primarily of those many who are dying for the Faith today. Yet many more Christians live in constant danger. According to reliable estimates, more than 200 million Christians in 60 countries around the world face some form of restriction on their faith.[2]

Persecution is happening today on a massive scale, and the perpetrators are from everywhere on the globe. They draw their motivation from a wide range of ideologies, from materialistic communism to radical Islam. They charge Christians with crimes such as sedition and blasphemy. Persecution is taking place in Iraq, Syria, Pakistan, India, China, Nigeria, Sudan, North Korea, and many other lands. It is happening in plain sight. Sometimes the persecutors brazenly post video footage of the execution of Christians on social media.

---

[1] Pope Francis, Address at the World Meeting of the Popular Movements in the City of Santa Cruz, Bolivia, July 9, 2015.

[2] From a report published by the British Secret Service, MI6. See "200 million Christians in 60 countries subject to persecution," Catholic News Agency, June 19, 2007.

Yet it is hardly remarked upon in major media outlets. It is barely noticed by diplomats and heads of state. It is, in fact, treated as a political liability. Christian martyrs, it has been said, are too religious to excite the interest of the American left and too foreign to rouse the interest of the right. And so martyrs are abandoned to their fate, left to suffer alone. We see the truth in the observation of the poet W. H. Auden: "even the dreadful martyrdom must run its course / Anyhow in a corner, some untidy spot."[3]

Pope Francis has called all Christians to rise up, cry out, and demand an end to the genocide. The end of the genocide must begin with an end to the silence.

I intend this book to be an act of solidarity with those who today are suffering for the Christian faith. Solidarity is the principle of unity in a society that extends beyond mere self-interest. Nowhere is this principle more essential and more real than in the Church of Jesus Christ. Since I share the Faith of the martyrs, we are members of a single body. When they suffer, I suffer, too. If my right hand were injured, ailing, or bleeding, I would seek immediate help. With this book I am seeking attention and relief for my fellow Christians who are in dire need.

Martyrdom, as we shall see, has proven to be a constant in the life of the Church. The Second Vatican Council confirmed that it always will be.

---

[3] W. H. Auden, "Musee des Beaux Arts," *Collected Poems* (New York: Random House, 1976), 147.

Since Jesus, the Son of God, manifested his charity by laying down his life for us, so too no one has greater love than he who lays down his life for Christ and his brothers. From the earliest times, then, some Christians have been called upon—and some will always be called upon—to give the supreme testimony of this love to all men, but especially to persecutors. The Church, then, considers martyrdom as an exceptional gift and as the fullest proof of love. By martyrdom a disciple is transformed into an image of his Master by freely accepting death for the salvation of the world—as well as his conformity to Christ in the shedding of his blood. Though few are presented such an opportunity, nevertheless all must be prepared to confess Christ before men. They must be prepared to make this profession of faith even in the midst of persecutions, which will never be lacking to the Church, in following the way of the cross.[4]

Martyrdom may be constant, and it may be inevitable. But that does not mean we should allow it to take place without consequence and unremarked. Every injustice should rouse us to speak more loudly and effectively for justice.

In my country, the United States, we have recently suffered some setbacks in the area of religious liberty, and these too must be addressed. Nevertheless, we still enjoy relatively

---

4 Second Vatican Council, Dogmatic Constitution on the Church *Lumen Gentium* (November 21, 1964), n. 42.

plenteous freedom to worship as we wish. How blessed we are that we can celebrate the Eucharist, honor the Trinity, proclaim Christ truly Risen—and then leave our churches in peace and security.

Meanwhile, many—and by many I mean many thousands—of our co-religionists cannot attend Mass without worrying that one of the cars parked nearby will explode. Many cannot gather on Sunday without wondering whether this is the day the militia will surround the church and set it on fire.

Knowing what we know, we cannot rest content. We must make a commitment to live in solidarity with those Christians who are suffering in our time. They are offering their lives for us. Their blood is seed for our children's Church. What are we doing for them?

May the writing of this book, and your reading of it, serve as a beginning.

Introduction
The Crime Called Christianity

What was the crime of the early Christians?

We tend to think of the Roman Era as the Age of Martyrs. We know that not long after the Church was born it was outlawed by the Roman Empire. Active persecution began in the first Christian century and continued intermittently into the fourth. We don't know the precise number of those who died rather than renounce their faith. Scholars differ on the calculus, but the persecution was extensive enough for the Romans to be remembered as much in history for making martyrs as for making aqueducts.

Imperial and local authorities promulgated the anti-Christian laws as if the cohesion of their society depended upon their mercilessness.

The centuries of Rome's imperial power correspond almost exactly to the Church's first formative years. Rome's power, moreover, extended over much of the known world. The lands it did not rule it still dominated economically and culturally. There was a temple to the emperor's genius built on the far shores of India. If Rome wanted a particular group to feel its wrath, its members might run far, but they could not hide for long.

The status of Christians in the first-century world seemed a rather precise fulfillment of Jesus' prediction: "If they persecuted me, they will persecute you" (John 15:20).

But the question remains: What exactly was the crime for which the martyrs were killed?

The Romans had a longstanding legal tradition and their rulers were required at least to pay lip service to its precedents, even as they confronted a new phenomenon that they viewed as a threat to their self-satisfaction.

The task of finding such a precedent fell to the emperor named Nero.

Nero hardly needs an introduction. He is the kind of historical villain who resists the most ambitious efforts of revisionist historians. He was so cruel, self-absorbed, and power-mad that it is impossible to rehabilitate his reputation by accentuating the positive.

He murdered his mother, Agrippina, in the year 59. A few years later, he had his first wife, Octavia, executed. It is reported that Nero himself kicked his second wife, Poppaea, to death while she was pregnant with their second child. He likely had his brother poisoned. Rather than attend to tedious matters of state, he amused himself by playing his lyre, writing poetry, or acting in pornographic public shows.

Nero had inherited an empire that was prosperous and at peace, thanks to the efforts of his forebears. Early in the century, Augustus had secured the borders and suppressed piracy on the high seas. The Roman military was well disciplined and feared throughout the world. To the capital city flowed taxes and tribute from distant lands.

The Roman people had abundant leisure. They could live comfortably off the labors of men and women whom their ancestors had conquered.

Nero was a living symbol of the decadence of his generation. His appetites were voracious and he indulged them. Most people were too busy indulging their own desires to notice. But he almost went too far, in the year 64, when he (according to most historical accounts) set fire to a large swath of the city in order to make room for his new palace, which he called the Golden House.

The citizens murmured, and they blamed Nero for the loss of life and property in what was then the worst fire in their city's history.

Nero needed to provide a distraction and find a way to shift the blame away from himself. His ideal candidates would be a detested minority—people powerless, disinclined to fight back, and unlikely to gain allies.

He blamed the Christians, whose religion the Roman people viewed as an Eastern religious cult, newly arrived in the city. Yet he could not risk putting them on trial for arson, because then their innocence might become apparent. Remember: the Romans valued the rule of law.

Since he could not make a case for arson, Nero had the Christians tried on another charge. And what was the crime of those first Roman Christians?

They were charged, according to the Roman historian

Tacitus, with "hatred of humanity."[1] And they were tried, convicted, and executed.

Nero tried to distract people from the injustice by turning the Christians' executions into extravagant public entertainment. He threw a party and invited everyone to attend. Then, at nightfall, he doused the Christians in pitch and set them on fire to light up the celebration. He dressed them up in the skins of animals and sent them into an arena to face animal predators.

The Romans could do such things to criminals who were convicted of the crime of "hatred of humanity."

It must have seemed a curious charge to the Christians. We have no trial transcripts, but surely they responded that they hated no one. They followed a Master whose New Commandment was to love without stinting and without exception. Yet in Rome they were identified with hatred—and so they were hated—and hated to death.

Such charges could stick because the Christians opposed what had become Rome's new morality—its routine adultery and easy divorce, its indolence and abuse of slave labor, its drunkenness and sadistic entertainments, its abortion and infanticide. To do these things was simply to live as a normal Roman, which was by earthly standards the pinnacle of humanity. To oppose such actions, then, was hatred of humanity.

---

[1] Tacitus, *Annals* 15.44.

All of that took place a long time ago in a land across the sea. It was then the Age of Martyrs; and many people believe that the Age of Martyrs is past.

But it is not. In fact, more people died for the Christian faith in the twentieth century than in all the other centuries combined. The mass killings of believers—for the simple fact of their faith—began with the Armenian Genocide and continued through the Soviet pogroms, the Spanish Civil War, the Nazi extermination camps, and China's Cultural Revolution. The pace has hardly slowed in our current century; and now the executioners post videos of their atrocities online to make a public spectacle of each death, just as Nero did.

I learned this hard truth when I was a very young priest. In the years 1969–1979 it was my privilege to serve the Church at the Vatican Congregation for the Clergy. Though our purview was the whole Church, there were large areas of the world where we had only intermittent communication—sometimes conveyed by word of mouth through a chain of contacts.

The news was often distressing. In 1976 the Argentinian bishop Enrique Ángel Angelelli was assassinated. In Congo in 1977 Cardinal Émile Biayenda was abducted and killed. In the Ukraine the martyrs included clergy, religious, and laity.[2] We heard similar stories from throughout the Soviet Bloc,

---

[2] For a full account, see Svitlana Hurkina and Rev. Andriy Mykhaleyko, eds., *To the Light of Resurrection through the Thorns of Catacombs: The Underground Activity and Reemergence of the Ukrainian Greek Catholic Church* (L'viv: Ukrainian Catholic University Press, 2014).

from China, from Vietnam and Laos, and from Latin America. Sometimes we heard only a man's name and the fact of his disappearance. Sometimes we heard rumors of the death of a cleric, and that's all—no name.

Each death represented a unique act of heroism. Each death bore its own distinctive witness. Each death had its own chilling drama. And yet in broad outline the stories were the same. A Christian refused to remain silent in the face of oppression, injustice, routinized corruption, suppression of the truth, and restriction of religious practice. A Christian refused to recognize any of these conditions as "normal"—and so was put to death, as Christ had been put to death, for love of humanity.

Such love always looks like a threat to the Neros of the world. Christianity is the killjoy, the spoilsport that dares to tally the cost of a despot's vices or a society's sins. Even when Christians remain silent, their silence itself stands as an accusing witness. In the sixteenth century, Thomas More did nothing to oppose King Henry; moreover, he withdrew from public life so as not to cause scandal by his refusal of support. Yet King Henry could not endure More's silence and so had him beheaded.

In my years in the Vatican's office for clergy, I came to know that martyrdom was a never-ending story. I learned this from the survivors—of the Nazi regime, of the Spanish horror—who lived as refugees in Rome or passed through on pilgrimage. They were generally cheerful, though sometimes frail, and they often bore visible marks of their maiming and torture.

While still working in Rome I undertook two studies of history's martyrs, which I published as books, *The Forty Martyrs: New Saints of England and Wales* and *Fathers of the Church*. These figures inspired me in my daily work for the Church. I knew that, at every moment, I had brothers and sisters awaiting their sentence in some distant prison, wondering whether they had been forgotten, calling out to heaven for deliverance and strength. I joined my prayers to theirs. It gave me joy to know that some of the work I did was for their benefit.

That thought still gives me joy. I could not help but remember the martyrs—many years after my service in Rome—when Pope Benedict XVI elevated me to the College of Cardinals. It was November 20, 2010; and as he presented us with the symbols of our office, he told us the meaning of the red hat and vestments we would receive. They were meant to signify our readiness for martyrdom, our willingness to follow "Christ on the Cross and also, if necessary, *usque ad effusionem sanguinis.*"[3] The Latin words mean "even to the shedding of blood."

But the vocation to martyrdom is hardly peculiar to the rank of Cardinal. Most of those who have borne this witness—to the shedding of blood—were not Cardinals, or bishops, or priests, or deacons. They were ordinary believers who loved the Lord and could not deny him. They were men and women—and even children—who dared to resist the cruel fads and fashions of their age. They bore the baptismal dig-

---

[3] Pope Benedict XVI, Homily at the Ordinary Public Consistory for the Creation of New Cardinals, November 20, 2010.

nity of children of God. And that is the greatest dignity any of us can wish to possess.

I have titled this book *To the Martyrs*, and the name has a dual meaning. I want to echo the call of the Church Fathers, like Tertullian the North African who in 197 wrote his *Ad Martyras*—To the Martyrs—and Origen the Egyptian who just a few years later wrote his *Exhortation to Martyrdom*. They urged their contemporaries to be ready to suffer for the Faith. And we, too, must be ready. If recent history proves anything at all, it proves that persecution can come suddenly and unexpectedly, even in traditionally Christian lands.

But there is a second sense to my title. I want to dedicate this work "to the martyrs." I write it in honor of all those who have suffered for the Faith—and all those who are suffering today—those whose stories I have heard and those whose stories are known only to God. They are numerous indeed. According to the Pew Research Center's ongoing study on religious liberty, Christians were in 2013 penalized or harassed in various ways in 102 countries.

What the world judges to be their crime, God reckons as faithfulness. What the world sees as hatred, we know to be the purest love.

Pope Francis put the matter bluntly in a recent homily: "There are . . . more martyrs in the Church today than there were in the first century."[4] This book is for them.

---

4 Pope Francis, Homily, Mass at Casa Santa Marta, June 30, 2014.

CHAPTER 1
The Supreme Testimony

"Martyrdom," said Pope Francis, "is the supreme testimony."[1]

It is the most vivid and most credible summary of the Gospel. Martyrs are Christians who take up the cross, as Jesus did. They vividly fulfill the condition of discipleship laid down by the Lord himself (Matthew 16:24; see also 10:38). They assume the role of Jesus on Calvary. Their death is a proclamation, even when the victim utters no words at the end. And no testimony to faith in Christ could be more compelling. In martyrdom the servant willingly identifies with the Master and consents to dying the same sort of death as he died, suffering the same injustice and humiliation.

Sermons provide a sort of testimony, and so do books, pamphlets, rallies, and websites. Such public witness is worthy of praise. But the martyr's testimony is greater and altogether more compelling. It is sealed with blood. The sociologist Rodney Stark, a professed agnostic, rightly called it the most valuable testimony conceivable.

> By voluntarily accepting torture and death rather than defecting, a person sets the highest imaginable

---

[1] Pope Francis, Homily, Mass at Casa Santa Marta, May 11, 2015.

value upon a religion and communicates the value to others . . . Christian martyrs typically had the opportunity to display their steadfastness to large numbers of other Christians, and the value of Christianity they thereby communicated often deeply impressed pagan observers as well.[2]

By their death martyrs tell the world, beginning with their persecutors, that Christian faith is worth the price, no matter how high.

From the very beginning of Christianity, the Church has singled out the act of martyrdom for special honor. Saint Stephen the deacon is the first Christian to die for the Faith and his story occupies a large portion (two chapters) of the narrative of the Acts of the Apostles. Other books of the New Testament, the Letter to the Hebrews and the Book of Revelation, also pay homage to those who have suffered for the sake of Jesus' name.

Tradition confirms what we see in Scripture. The feasts of the martyrs were the first dates—after the solemnities of Jesus Christ—to be commemorated in the Church's calendar. The anniversary of a martyr's death was known as his or her *dies natalis* (birthday) and celebrated with due festivity in the liturgy and in Christian homes.

The Church gave honor even to the bodily remains of the martyrs. After the lions had done their work—or the flames,

---

[2] Rodney Stark, *The Rise of Christianity* (San Francisco: HarperCollins, 1997), 163–189.

or the gladiators—Christians lovingly gathered what was left of the martyrs' bodies. Over time they encased the martyrs' remains in reliquaries made of precious metals and gems. They built churches over them, too. Some of those churches are today among the grandest in the world: Saint Peter's Basilica in Rome, for example, and the Basilica of Saint Paul Outside the Walls.

The Church also preserved the accounts of each martyr's death. Christians paid to obtain the court transcripts of the martyrs' interrogations, and then published these as the *Acta Martyrum*, the "acts of the martyrs." Those present at the death of martyrs were encouraged to record, in detail, what they had seen and heard.

The names of the great martyrs were remembered, at every Mass, in the Eucharistic prayer of the Western Church. We still remember them today: *John and Paul, Cosmas and Damian . . . Ignatius, Alexander, Marcellinus, Peter, Felicity, Perpetua, Agatha, Lucy, Agnes, Cecilia, Anastasia.*

By recalling those names, the Church amplifies the "supreme testimony" of women and men who lived long ago and whose lives were—except for their dramatic ending—quite ordinary. They were civil servants, physicians, soldiers, mothers, wives, daughters, students, parish priests.

They placed the highest value imaginable on the Christian faith, and the Church in turn has placed the highest value imaginable on their testimony. Let us look more closely at their vocation, to understand the Church's teaching on martyrdom: what it is and what it is not.

When Pope Francis used the phrase "supreme testimony," he was invoking the constant faith of Christians as it is expressed in the *Catechism of the Catholic Church*.

> Martyrdom is the supreme witness given to the truth of the faith: it means bearing witness even unto death. The martyr bears witness to Christ who died and rose, to whom he is united by charity. He bears witness to the truth of the faith and of Christian doctrine. He endures death through an act of fortitude. "Let me become the food of the beasts, through whom it will be given me to reach God."[3]

The Catechism discusses martyrdom in its section dedicated to the Church's ordinary "transmission of the faith in words and deeds."[4] Christian witness takes many forms, ranging from quiet conversation through public proclamation—but martyrdom stands at the far end of that range, as the supreme testimony.

Most Christians will not be called to testify that way. Yet the martyrs establish a standard of self-giving against which all Christians should measure their own. The martyrs give everything they have—they give their lives—for the sake of

---

[3] CCC 2473. The embedded quotation is from Saint Ignatius of Antioch, *Letter to the Romans* 4.1.

[4] CCC 2742.

Jesus Christ. They invite us all to ask ourselves how much we give and how much we hold back.

The martyrs, then, are a measure; and as such they have always been held up for public veneration. In the Church's early days there was no formal process for declaring a Christian to be a "saint" or "blessed." It happened by popular acclamation. Believers instinctively honored the martyrs in an extraordinary way. And veneration was an almost exclusive privilege of the martyrs. We know of very few *non*-martyr saints from the first three centuries.

The process for canonization developed gradually over time. As the authority to declare saints was reserved to the pope, the requirements for proving a candidate's sanctity became more stringent, the investigations more vigorous.

Yet, even then, martyrs were treated in a way that was different from other candidates—and this continues even to the present day. The Church normally requires the evidence of two miracles attributed to a candidate's post-mortem intercession: one miracle for beatification and another for canonization. Martyrs, though, may be declared blessed without a miracle, and they need only one in order to be canonized.

Pope Saint John Paul II, as he prepared to mark the turn of the millennium, called all the churches of the world to cultivate a deeper appreciation for the testimony of those who have died for the Faith.

At the end of the second millennium, the Church has once again become a Church of martyrs. . . . This witness must not be forgotten. The Church of the first centuries, although facing considerable organizational difficulties, took care to write down in special martyrologies the witness of the martyrs. . . . In our own century the martyrs have returned, many of them nameless, "unknown soldiers" as it were of God's great cause. As far as possible, their witness should not be lost to the Church.[5]

Having come of age in wartime Poland, John Paul experienced the persecution of the Church under both the Nazi and Soviet regimes. He witnessed firsthand the return of the Church to the conditions of the Roman era: operating underground, fearing denunciation, grieving almost continuously over the loss of friends, neighbors, and family members.

Yet he recognized also that there were significant differences in the modern persecutions. Sometimes the persecutors were themselves nominal Christians. And they preferred, in many cases, that the execution of Christians should take place out of the public eye. They were keen to rid themselves of difficult opponents, but they knew that martyrdom could galvanize Christian opposition. Thus, "difficult" Christians often simply "disappeared," taken by night from their homes.

John Paul and his successors have seen the need to adapt the canonization process to accommodate these conditions found in the modern totalitarian state.

---

[5] Pope Saint John Paul II, Apostolic Letter On Preparation for the Jubilee of the Year 2000 *Tertio Millennio Adveniente* (November 10, 1994), n. 37.

Since the eighteenth century at least, the Church has defined a martyr as someone who dies *in odium fidei*—because of hatred of the Faith. In 2006 Pope Benedict XVI affirmed that that condition had not changed. "What has changed," however, "are the cultural contexts of martyrdom." What has changed are the strategies of persecutors "that more and more seldom explicitly show their aversion to the Christian faith or to a form of conduct connected with the Christian virtues, but simulate different reasons, for example, of a political or social nature."[6]

Secular totalitarian states will not prosecute Christians on religious grounds, as the ancient Romans did. They won't ask people to enter temples and burn incense before idols. Instead, they demand that Christians compromise their morals, their sense of justice, their belief in human dignity and freedom, and their commitment to evangelize. They care little what believers do in private; but they criminalize any social or public expression of faith. Maximilian Kolbe and Jerzy Popiełuszko were arrested not simply for their religious affiliation, but because they spoke an inconvenient truth and dared to publish it abroad.

Some people have asked, then: Did these modern victims die *in odium fidei*? Did they die because their persecutors hated the Catholic faith—or were they singled out rather for their political views?

These questions can be difficult to answer, as they touch

---

[6] Pope Benedict XVI, Letter to the Participants of the Plenary Session of the Congregation for the Causes of the Saints, April 24, 2006.

upon the interior dispositions—the deepest motivations—of both the persecutors and the martyrs. Pope Benedict insisted that "the motive that impels" the martyrs—"their source and their model"—must be Jesus Christ. The persecutors, for their part, must show clear evidence of contempt for the Faith, either in its objects or its principles. "It is likewise necessary," he said, "directly or indirectly but always in a morally certain way, to ascertain the *odium fidei* [hatred of the faith] of the persecutor. If this element is lacking, there would be no true martyrdom."[7]

People sometimes grow impatient because of the Church's caution in examining such questions. They grieve the loss of life and they see recognition of sainthood as a public vindication of the martyr.

Again, however, the Church must avoid being used for political ends—and also must protect the martyrs from political exploitation. The martyrs belong to Christ, not to a party, faction, or protest movement. They will be remembered for their sacrifice long after the temporal circumstances of their martyrdom have vanished.

Martyrdom should be admired, and it may be desired, but it should not be sought. It is a particular vocation received by a few.

Apart from the Bible, the earliest known account of an

---

[7] Ibid.

individual Christian's execution is the second-century text known as *The Martyrdom of Polycarp*. It describes the trial and death of the Bishop of Smyrna, who had been a disciple of the Apostle John. The text was set down by an eyewitness and addressed to the local Church in Smyrna as well as "all the congregations of the Holy and Catholic Church in every place."[8]

Like the account of Saint Stephen in the Acts of the Apostles, *The Martyrdom of Polycarp* became a universal template for Christian behavior in the face of persecution. Here was a man trained by the Apostles, a man of unquestionable authority, answering the standard questions of a Roman interrogation. He answered them with firmness and with good humor. He shows respect for temporal power, but refuses to exalt it above Christ. He even offers to make an appointment to instruct his inquisitor in the Faith.

He is condemned, of course, and his execution proceeds by fits and starts. The torturers try to burn him alive, but the flames do not kill the bishop. Finally, he is run through with a blade.

But there is a curious passage early in the narrative. It describes how Polycarp, when he first realizes he is in danger, seeks refuge in a farmhouse not far from the city. There he devotes himself to prayer, and God reveals to him that he must die for the Faith.

Meanwhile, back in Smyrna, a man named Quintus pres-

---

[8] Here and in the paragraphs that follow, I use the translation of *The Martyrdom of Polycarp* found in the nineteenth-century Ante-Nicene Fathers series. I have modernized the language.

ents himself proudly to the authorities as a Christian. He is full of bluster and the appearance of courage; and the governor obliges by condemning him to be devoured by wild beasts. When he sees the animals, however, he changes his mind, renounces the Faith, and agrees to offer sacrifice to the idols of the Roman pantheon. The author of the *Martyrdom* speaks for the Church as he remarks: "we do not commend those who give themselves up to suffering, as the Gospel does not teach to do so."

Indeed, as much as the Gospel praises those who suffer for the Faith, the Lord himself counsels: "When they persecute you in one town, flee to the next" (Matthew 10:23). The first Christians took his advice and evaded capture when they could (see, for example, Acts 8:1, 9:25, 14:6).

It was persecution, in fact, that spread the Gospel from one place to another, as the disciples fled from city to city. Christianity would not have reached Antioch if the disciples had not been forced to flee from Jerusalem. Persecution, though it seemed to be a setback, turned out to be God's providential way of ensuring the growth of the Church.

Nevertheless, the Apostles were able to discern when the time was right for their martyrdom. According to an ancient tradition, all but one of them (Saint John) died as martyrs; and even John suffered tortures that should have killed him and certainly left their marks. The earliest Roman traditions tell of Saint Peter attempting to flee, only to encounter Jesus on the road out of town. Seeing Christ, Peter knew he must return to die in Rome.

Martyrdom is a vocation. Christians may not grasp it for themselves. But when God calls, faith requires a positive response. Like any vocation, martyrdom must respect the conditions set by the Church, and it should be discerned in prayer and tested by wise spiritual counsel.

The story of Quintus should remain forever a cautionary tale for Christians. Martyrs are called, not self-appointed. They are brave, but they know their weakness and vulnerability. They recognize their fears, but they subordinate all earthly fears to the fear of the Lord.

Martyrdom is a vocation and a grace. Christians prepare themselves for martyrdom—and correspond to God's grace—through the ordinary path of Christian life: prayer, sacrifice, and charity. One who hopes to end his life as Christ did should strive always to live his life as Christ did. If we would imitate Christ in the end, we should renew our efforts to follow him day after day.

God gives the grace, and only God knows how much preparation each person will require. In recent years we have witnessed the astonishing phenomenon of non-Christians who chose to die beside their friends who were Christians. In February 2015, soldiers of the Islamic State beheaded twenty-one men on a beach in Libya. Twenty of the victims were Coptic Christians. The lone exception was a man so moved by the example of his fellow prisoners that he uttered an unforgettable line: "Their God is my God."

The Church has always held that those who suffer death for the sake of the Faith die as Christian martyrs, even if they have not received the Sacrament of Baptism. They are baptized by their death. They are saved. They are saints. Tradition calls this the "Baptism of Blood."[9]

Nothing shows so beautifully, memorably, and clearly the profound truth about martyrdom. It is a call, a gift, and a mystery. It is not to be sought, but to be accepted if it is given.

⚜

The Holy Father spoke of martyrdom as "testimony," and that is indeed the literal meaning of the Greek *martyria*—the word we translate to English as "martyrdom."

Today its primary sense is religious. We apply it to the act of dying for a transcendent cause. In the first century, however, it was an ordinary term with workaday associations. *Martyria* was the testimony given by a witness (*martys*) in a court of law.

For the early Christians it became the preferred term for a public proclamation of the Gospel, especially one given before a hostile audience. Christians living in the world were often, it seemed, on trial for their beliefs. They were called to give testimony—to give an account for their hope when their neighbors were despairing, or to give reasons for their moral discipline, which was demanding but secured their happiness.

---

[9] See CCC 1258 and 1281.

The most persuasive witness of all—the most convincing and convicting witness of all—was the willingness to die rather than deny, betray, or compromise the Faith of the Church. So the Greek word for "witness" became synonymous with a courageous Christian death. And the martyrs became the supreme measure of all other testimony. By their death they told the whole truth about Christ, and nothing but the truth.

CHAPTER 2
Israel and the Inevitability of Persecution

The world is fallen. It is not as it should be. According to Christian dogma, this universal condition of disorder can be traced back to an original sin—a fall from the grace and peace intended for humanity.

The novelist G.K. Chesterton observed that original sin "is the only part of Christian theology which can really be proved."[1] The irrefutable evidence is in the news and on our city streets, where we see the sad results of the suffering that human beings visit upon their neighbors—violence, exploitation, envy, theft, and hatred. The evidence is also in every home and every heart, though its presence can be subtle and hidden.

Christianity begins with the acknowledgment of this predicament and proceeds to an admission of human helplessness to overcome the tendency to sin. Only by God's grace, given through Jesus Christ, can we begin to experience the justice and peace intended for us in creation.

Even in our hobbled state, however, God equipped each

---

[1] G. K. Chesterton, *Orthodoxy* (New York: Image, 1959), 15.

of us with a conscience to know right behavior from wrong. God revealed the moral law to Israel, moreover, and established them as a chosen people to model his justice and peace to all other nations. "Israel is my first-born," God said to Moses (Exodus 4:22); and as the eldest child Israel was to be a model and teacher, "a light to the nations" (Isaiah 42:6, 49:6, 51:4).

The problem is—and it always will be—that many people profit from the world's disorder. Many people gain vast power and wealth by exploiting the weakness of the fallen human race. For such people, disorder is the established "order" that must be protected at all cost. They see conscience and justice, then, as a threat, an enemy that demands opposition.

And so biblical religion has always arrived as a peculiar thing in the world. It is the clear, resounding word of the Lord spoken amid societies that are chaotic and confused. Because it is peculiar, it is usually treated as something alien and dangerous. It is persecuted.

The constancy of persecution is a dominant theme in Jesus' preaching; but the reality predates him. God's chosen people were often misunderstood. They endured enslavement, conquest, occupation, and exile. Israel's overlords saw that the people derived their strong national identity from common morals, customs, and worship; and so they tried to weaken or shatter the tradition. The Assyrians, Babylonians, Persians, Greeks, and Romans tried this in different ways, with varying degrees of "success." Fairly typical is the purge described in the First Book of Maccabees:

The books of the law which they [the Greeks] found they tore to pieces and burned with fire. Where the book of the covenant was found in the possession of any one, or if any one adhered to the law, the decree of the king condemned him to death. They kept using violence against Israel, against those found month after month in the cities. And on the twenty-fifth day of the month they offered sacrifice on the altar which was upon the altar of burnt offering. According to the decree, they put to death the women who had their children circumcised, and their families and those who circumcised them; and they hung the infants from their mothers' necks. But many in Israel stood firm and were resolved in their hearts not to eat unclean food. They chose to die rather than to be defiled by food or to profane the holy covenant; and they did die. (1 Maccabees 1:56–63)

Were the Greeks truly offended by the Jews' custom of circumcising male children? Or by their refusal to eat pork or shellfish?

No, of course they weren't. In no way did Jewish worship hinder the Greeks in their conquests. What offended them was the Jews' claim to have possession of a law from the one true God—a law that, if true, would be binding for all the world.

The law of Israel seemed a threat because it seemed plausible. It made for a good life, a clean life, a happy life. Moreover, the Jews showed that they would "rather die," as the Biblical narrative tells us, than violate the law. They would be happier while tortured than their persecutors were while sinning. That is a credible testimony to the power of God's law.

The Bible's Old Testament speaks often of persecution. The Psalms cry out to heaven for deliverance from "enemies and persecutors" (Psalm 31:15). Again, however, the most detailed account of systematic persecution of the Jews is set down in the books of Maccabees, written in the first century before Christ.

The Second Book of Maccabees is best known for its story of seven brothers who are executed, one by one, for their refusal to eat food prohibited by the law of Moses (see 2 Maccabees 7). The young men are tortured horrifically. The king orders his executioner to cut out their tongues, then their scalps, and then cut off their hands and feet. Finally the victims are fried in a pan till they are dead.

Their mother watches the torments of each son and urges them all to remain faithful to God. Each of the sons makes a statement of faith before losing his tongue. Two of them profess their hope in the resurrection and restoration of the body, and so they show contempt for the threats of their torturers. The fourth son says: "One cannot but choose to die at the hands of men and to cherish the hope that God gives of being raised again by him." Finally, the mother, too, is killed.

The story was carefully preserved so that future generations could find inspiration in it. Jews have looked to that unnamed family as a symbol of defiant resistance. Christians, from the very beginnings of the Church, have seen the mother and her sons as biblical types—real historical figures who foreshadow a later fulfillment. They prefigured the first generations of Christian martyrs. Indeed, the early Christians honored the Maccabean victims themselves as martyrs. Their bodily remains were eventually transported to Rome, where they are venerated in the Church of Saint Peter in Chains.

God's people experienced much persecution and so they became expert in understanding the psychology of their tormentors. The Old Testament Book of Wisdom devotes an entire chapter (Chapter 2) to a soliloquy in the voice of a persecutor.

The passage is fascinating because it begins at a point far from any thoughts of oppressing other people. It begins, instead, with a denial of any transcendent meaning or purpose to life.

Short and sorrowful is our life,
and there is no remedy when a man comes to his end,
and no one has been known to return from Hades.
Because we were born by mere chance,
and hereafter we shall be as though we had never been;
because the breath in our nostrils is smoke,
and reason is a spark kindled by the beating of our hearts.

When it is extinguished, the body will turn to ashes,
and the spirit will dissolve like empty air.
Our name will be forgotten in time
and no one will remember our works;
our life will pass away like the traces of a cloud,
and be scattered like mist
that is chased by the rays of the sun
and overcome by its heat.
For our allotted time is the passing of a shadow,
and there is no return from our death,
because it is sealed up and no one turns back.

Since life is short and ends definitively with death, the speaker presses on to advocate a life given entirely to pleasure. Since he recognizes no god and fears no judgment he places no limits on the indulgence of his desires.

Come, therefore, let us enjoy the good things that exist,
and make use of the creation to the full as in youth.
Let us take our fill of costly wine and perfumes,
and let no flower of spring pass by us.
Let us crown ourselves with rosebuds before they wither.
Let none of us fail to share in our revelry,
everywhere let us leave signs of enjoyment,
because this is our portion, and this our lot.

But then his reverie—so far entirely self-absorbed—takes a strange turn and considers another person. He considers that "other," however, not as an object of care or concern, but as a target for oppression.[2]

> Let us oppress the righteous poor man;
> let us not spare the widow
> nor regard the gray hairs of the aged.
> But let our might be our law of right,
> for what is weak proves itself to be useless.
> Let us lie in wait for the righteous man,
> because he is inconvenient to us and opposes our actions;
> he reproaches us for sins against the law,
> and accuses us of sins against our training.
> He professes to have knowledge of God,
> and calls himself a child of the Lord.
> He became to us a reproof of our thoughts;
> the very sight of him is a burden to us,
> because his manner of life is unlike that of others,
> and his ways are strange.
> We are considered by him as something base,
> and he avoids our ways as unclean;
> he calls the last end of the righteous happy,
> and boasts that God is his father.
> Let us see if his words are true,

---

[2] The passage from Wisdom is reminiscent also of the famous "Man of Sorrows" oracle of the Prophet Isaiah 53:3–9: "But he was wounded for our transgressions, he was bruised for our iniquities; upon him was the chastisement that made us whole, and with his stripes we are healed. . . . witnessed firsthand witnessed firsthand He was oppressed, and he was afflicted, yet he opened not his mouth, like a lamb that is led to the slaughter." Both Scriptures are traditionally invoked as prophecies of the Passion of Jesus Christ.

and let us test what will happen at the end of his life;

for if the righteous man is God's son, he will help him,

and will deliver him from the hand of his adversaries.

Let us test him with insult and torture,

that we may find out how gentle he is,

and make trial of his forbearance.

Let us condemn him to a shameful death,

for, according to what he says, he will be protected.

Note that the righteous man's "offense" is not so much any word or deed directed at the oppressor. It is, rather, *his very righteousness* that gives offense. By his life he reminds the wicked that goodness is possible—that it is more noble—and that it is more admirable. He reminds them, too—through the example of his piety—of the uncomfortable fact of God's existence and the eventual judgment of every human being.

A righteous life is a reproach to the wicked, a reminder of what they should be doing and proof that it can be done. The Book of Wisdom later goes on to observe that "wickedness is a cowardly thing, condemned by its own testimony; distressed by conscience, it has always exaggerated the difficulties" (Wisdom 17:11). Thus the wicked, tormented in conscience, face a choice: either to end the immoral life they've been living—or end the witness of the righteous life that makes them feel "distressed."

Persecution was a recurrent hardship in the life of ancient Israel—and in the lives of the Old Testament heroes. The prophets bore messages from God, but these were rarely welcomed by kings or by the people. The prophets were often driven into hiding or exile. They had to endure long stretches without food. Some were murdered because of the hard truth of their oracles.

Biblical religion is difficult to bear because it is true. If it were merely peculiar, it would be merely scorned and mocked, like membership in a flat-earth society. The problem is that it is *peculiar because it is true*—and so much in this world is given over to falsehood. Many people are deeply and personally invested in lies and will go to great lengths to protect their investments.

That is why the Greek conquerors could not abide the presence of the Jews who wanted to live by the law and offer the proper sacrifice to God. That is why, in the Book of Wisdom, the wicked cannot rest until the righteous are dead.

A generation ago, the Venerable Fulton Sheen observed: "The wicked fear the good, because the good are a constant reproach to their consciences. The ungodly like religion in the same way that they like lions, either dead or behind bars; they fear religion when it breaks loose and begins to challenge their consciences."[3]

Such is the religion of the martyrs.

---

[3] Fulton J. Sheen, *Life of Christ* (New York: Image, 2008), 164.

CHAPTER 3

"You Shall Be My Witnesses":
Martyrdom in the New Testament

Saint Stephen was among the first seven men to be set apart as deacons in the Church. In the first history of the Church, the New Testament Acts of the Apostles, he is described as "a man full of faith" who, after his ordination, "did great wonders and signs among the people" (Acts 6:5, 8). He preaches and teaches and he gives his life to service in the Church.

Today, however, Stephen is most remembered not for pioneering the diaconate, but rather for his death. Since the early days of the Church, in fact, Christians have honored Stephen with the title *Protomartyr*. It is a Greek compound meaning "first martyr," and it belongs to Stephen alone.

Stephen is the first disciple of Jesus to die for the Faith. The enormity of that event, for the first Christians, is evident from the coverage it is given in the Acts of the Apostles. Saint Luke wrote the Acts as a history of the Church's first generation. The key moments in the drama were events that established the identity of the Church for all time. And what are those events: the descent of the Holy Spirit at Pentecost; the conversion of Saul the Persecutor; the first doctrinal controversy and its settlement at the Council of Jerusalem—and Stephen's martyrdom.

Stephen's story occupies an entire chapter and portions of the chapters before and after. In a typical English translation, it takes up almost a tenth of the entire book. While the marvels of his ministry are mentioned in passing, the focus of the story is Stephen's last act of public preaching, in which he held the religious leaders in Jerusalem responsible for the death of Jesus—and guilty of outrages against God.

> Now when they heard these things they were enraged, and they ground their teeth against him. But he, full of the Holy Spirit, gazed into heaven and saw the glory of God, and Jesus standing at the right hand of God; and he said, "Behold, I see the heavens opened, and the Son of man standing at the right hand of God." But they cried out with a loud voice and stopped their ears and rushed together upon him. Then they cast him out of the city and stoned him. . . . And as they were stoning Stephen, he prayed, "Lord Jesus, receive my spirit." And he knelt down and cried with a loud voice, "Lord, do not hold this sin against them." And when he had said this, he fell asleep.

Stephen's death would serve forever as a "prototype" of the supreme testimony for the Faith. He is rightly called Protomartyr, as his death foreshadows the vocation of many

Christians in the centuries to come. Even though he is "first," however, his martyrdom points us still further back to another, earlier case.

It points us back to Jesus.

Saint Luke, who wrote the Acts of the Apostles, also wrote the third Gospel in our New Testament canon.

In Acts, Stephen's death is essential to the story. It marks the beginning of the first great persecution of the Church. It introduces the character of Saul as an arch-persecutor—who later became an eminent Apostle. It models Christian fearlessness in confronting a hostile culture.

In the Gospel, of course, it is Jesus' death that dominates the story.

Since ancient times, readers of both of Luke's books have pointed out how similar are the accounts of the death of Jesus and the death of Stephen. In both cases, there is a conspiracy against the victim. In both stories, we find a trial and interrogation, a condemnation and brutal execution. In both cases, the victims forgive their persecutors; and then both victims commit their spirit to God. Both Jesus and Stephen die at the hands of a frenzied mob in the holy city, Jerusalem.

The similarities are important because they show us the reason for Stephen's prominence in the history of the early Church. He was a prototype *not simply because he was killed*, but because his life represented a rather exact "imitation of

Christ." To the end he was not doing anything new or innovative. He was following a pattern already established. He was following the footsteps of his Master along the way of the cross.

Indeed, Jesus had made it clear that persecution would be an inevitable part of the Christian experience. As the disciples imitated Jesus and shared his life, they would surely share his suffering. "A servant is not greater than his master. If they persecuted me, they will persecute you; if they kept my word, they will keep yours also" (John 15:20).

Jesus said, moreover, that the persecuted would be "blessed" (Matthew 5:10–12). He listed persecution not among the *losses* suffered by believers, but among the *gains* they would enjoy (Mark 10:30)!

The Gospels show us that Jesus did not look for trouble; but he did speak the truth, and the truth affected the wicked in exactly the same way it affected the wicked described in the Old Testament Book of Wisdom. From the time of his birth Jesus faced opposition: from Herod the Great, and then Herod's heir, from the Pharisees and the priests, from Pontius Pilate and the Romans.

It is something he was prepared for. He foresaw the events and warned his disciples of what was coming: "Behold, we are going up to Jerusalem; and the Son of man will be delivered to the chief priests and scribes, and they will condemn him to death, and deliver him to the Gentiles to be mocked and scourged and crucified" (Matthew 20:18–19). He knew his vocation, and he was true to it. "When the days drew near for him to be received up, he set his face to go to Jerusalem" (Luke 9:51).

At his trial before Pilate he spoke of his purpose as testimony, as witness: "For this I was born, and for this I have come into the world, to bear witness to the truth" (John 18:37). In bearing witness, of course, he used the Greek word that is the root of our word "martyr."

He had come into the world for testimony; and his supreme testimony would be his death.

So much of his previous testimony—his preaching and counsel—had made the matter very clear. Anyone who reads the tenth chapter of Saint Matthew's Gospel will see how the theme of persecution was central to his message. At the beginning of the chapter Jesus calls twelve disciples to have special authority in the Church. He tells them where to go, and what to do and say. He tells them what they should carry as they travel. This is his most detailed and practical instruction for Christian leadership and ministry. Yet already with verse fourteen he anticipates that some people will refuse his emissaries. He warns: "Behold, I send you out as sheep in the midst of wolves. . . . they will deliver you up to councils, and flog you in their synagogues, and you will be dragged before governors and kings for my sake, to bear testimony before them" (verses 17–18).

Not only kings and governors condemn the disciples. Jesus goes on to predict that Christians would be oppressed, rejected, and betrayed by their own family members—and even delivered to death (verses 21–22, 35–36).

Yet the disciples should never give in to discouragement. The Holy Spirit will tell them what to say when they are questioned (verse 19). The Father will care for them when they are in duress (verses 29–32).

To know salvation in Jesus Christ is to share his life with the Father. It is to share in a life far greater than earthly life could ever be. Yet Jesus' earthly life ended with his crucifixion; and those who are saved should not be surprised if they, too, find themselves outcast and condemned. Jesus said: "He who does not take his cross and follow me is not worthy of me. He who finds his life will lose it, and he who loses his life for my sake will find it" (verses 38–39). Readiness for martyrdom, then, was not optional. It was essential.

Only at the end of this long seminar on persecution do we learn that Jesus "had finished instructing his twelve disciples" (Matthew 11:1).

Jesus was sending his disciples out "to bear testimony." Yet he spent relatively little time speaking to them about doctrine. Instead he steeled them to face opposition. He prepared them to give a witness that might be wordless. He prepared them for *martyria*—witness—culminating, perhaps, with the witness of martyrdom.

⚜

The disciples were well prepared. Besides the word of Jesus' instruction, they observed the example of Saint John the Baptist, who was put to death because he dared to defend

God's plan for marriage (see Mark 6:14–29).

What the twelve had received from Jesus, they passed on to their own disciples. We see the effectiveness of their teaching in the life and death of Saint Stephen. Nor was Stephen the last of his generation to give his life in testimony. "Herod the king laid violent hands upon some who belonged to the Church. He killed James the brother of John with the sword" (Acts 12:1–2) and others whose names we do not know (Acts 26:10).

By the end of the apostolic era, such witnesses must have been numerous. In the Book of Revelation John sees a vision of heaven and "the souls of those who had been slain for the word of God and for the witness they had borne" (6:9). He sees the earthly tyrants "drunk with the blood of the saints and the blood of the martyrs of Jesus" (17:6). John even mentions one victim by name, Antipas, and refers to him as a "witness" (martyr) (2:12). Revelation 11:3–10 also seems to describe what had, by then, become the normal lot of those who preached in the name of Jesus. They are killed, their bodies left to rot in the street, "and those who dwell on the earth . . . rejoice over them and make merry and exchange presents, because these two prophets had been a torment to those who dwell on the earth."

The expectation diminished not at all in the following generation, the time of the Apostolic Fathers. But those Christians, too, were prepared, because they knew the story of Jesus Christ.

More than a century ago, one scholar defined the Gospels

as "passion narratives with an extended introduction."[1] And that's an accurate description. Jesus' whole life—as it was set down in the Gospels—was oriented toward the witness of his death. He was the grain of wheat that bore fruit only after death and burial (see John 12:24). His final witness—the supreme testimony—was the culmination and summary of his life.

The first generation of Christians heard that story, repeatedly, proclaimed in their liturgy. They heard the readings before they received Christ, the "grain of wheat," in the bread of the Eucharist. In receiving his life, they accepted it as their own. They shared his life. They imitated it to the end.

What had been a recurrent hardship in the Old Testament—persecution—became a central motif of the New Testament. In the Old Testament, the people prayed for persecution to pass. In the New Testament, Jesus revealed to the Church that persecution would last as long as the world. Indeed, it would be a mark of authenticity for his Church. The Church, like Christ, would be an almost universal irritant, afflicting the comfortable even as it comforted the afflicted. The Church, like Jesus Christ, would offer the witness of suffering as a prelude to glory.

---

[1] Martin Kähler, *The So-Called Historical Jesus and the Historic, Biblical Christ* (Philadelphia: Fortress Press, 1964), 80.

CHAPTER 4

Blood Is Seed:
The Martyrs of the Roman Era

Saint Ignatius of Antioch is one of the great figures of the ancient Church. He was bishop in the city where the disciples had first been called Christians (see Acts 11:26). In that office, he was the second successor to the Apostle Peter. Syrian Antioch, moreover, was one of the most important military and commercial centers in the Roman Empire.

His title and pedigree would have been enough to bring him to prominence in the Christian community in 107. His contemporary, Saint Polycarp of Smyrna, referred to him already as "the blessed Ignatius."

But Ignatius was revered not for his wise administration of the Church in Antioch, or for any miracles he performed, or for any homilies he preached. In fact, we know hardly anything about Ignatius's life before his final months on earth.

All that we know about Ignatius is what we can glean from seven letters that he wrote as he journeyed from Antioch to Rome. "Journeyed" is perhaps the wrong word. He was traveling as a condemned prisoner, under military escort, for the execution of his sentence in the capital city.

Ignatius looms large in Church history not because of his life or accomplishments, but because of his death. He died as a martyr.

His letters give us no clue about the crime for which he was condemned. Perhaps he faced the same charges as Nero's victims a generation before. The circumstances of his execution, however, seem strange. It must have cost a small fortune to transport him, with armed guards, across land and sea. Why didn't the authorities simply kill him in Antioch? In the case of Saint Paul, it was the Apostle's appeal to Caesar that required a trip to Rome. Ignatius, however, makes no such appeal. He accepts his sentence, and he is eager to have it carried out.

It is quite likely that his judge or prosecutors recognized the value of this particular case. Ignatius was an old man and longtime bishop; his name was well known by Christians everywhere. Antioch was an important city and Christian center; its bishop would have enjoyed a certain prominence. Such a criminal should die a most exemplary death—in the empire's capital. Such a criminal should be brought out and publicly shamed as he stopped in major cities along the way, like Smyrna and Troas in Asia Minor (modern Turkey).

If the Roman authorities wished to discourage the practice of Christianity—and it seems that they did—then Ignatius's final journey makes a sort of sense.

What's interesting is that his visibility seems to have had an effect very different from the one intended. When the entourage stopped, Ignatius took the opportunity to write letters—to the local church and nearby churches. He addressed Christians as if he had special authority over them, not simply because of his office, but rather because of his death sentence! He wore his condemnation not as a mark of shame but as a badge of honor. He spoke as if his imminent death conferred a retroactive authority on his words while still alive. Ignatius wrote seven letters during his two stops in Smyrna and Troas. Six are addressed to churches and one to Smyrna's young bishop, named Polycarp. The churches acknowledged the prisoner's special authority, and they carefully preserved the letters he left them.

The seven letters are important for historians because they reveal many of the ordinary concerns of Christians as the first century turned over to the second. Ignatius asserts both the divinity and the humanity of Jesus Christ. He speaks of Jesus' real presence in the Eucharist. He assumes that every local church has a three-tiered hierarchy, with one bishop, assisted by presbyters and deacons.

Ignatius worries about Church unity and acknowledges that heresies are already dividing Christians against one another. He urges the clergy and congregations to unite around the bishop.

Ignatius speaks authoritatively about many things. Yet he speaks hardly at all about himself. He doesn't mention anything about his past, not even a word about his arrest or trial. He shows no anxiety over leaving administrative "loose ends" in his church. He never seems to look back, only forward.

He sets his face like flint toward Rome, clear-eyed about what awaits him there. In one letter he imagines his execution—the lions grinding him in their teeth the way millers ground wheat into flour. He urges the Roman Christians to do nothing on his behalf, to make no appeals, plan no delays. He embraced his identity as martyr.

Yet he never—in all seven letters—uses the word "martyr" to describe himself or any other Christian who dies for the Faith. Thus, it seems, by 107, the Church had not yet advanced a single technical term to describe someone who witnessed to Christ by death. Nevertheless, what we today understand as martyrdom is the kind of testimony Ignatius desired to give.

"I shall willingly die for God," he wrote to the Romans, "if you do not hinder me. I beg you not to show an inopportune goodwill toward me. Let me become food for the wild beasts. . . . Permit me to be an imitator of the passion of my God. . . . It is better for me to die on behalf of Jesus Christ, than to reign over all the ends of the earth."[1]

Ignatius says repeatedly that he is in bonds for the sake of Jesus' name. He nowhere speaks as if his circumstances are unusual or unexpected. In fact, he seems to draw already from abundant history of persecution, though less than a century had passed since the Church was born on Pentecost.

It was the martyrdom of Stephen that had driven the disciples out of Jerusalem. From Stephen's death, the Church of Antioch was born—and the Faith of Ignatius and so many

---

[1] Saint Ignatius of Antioch, *Letter to the Romans* 4, 5, and 6.

others. Ignatius expected great things to come from his own death. And they did.

By the time of Ignatius it was considered a crime, in territories ruled by Rome, to practice Christianity. We see this more clearly in an exchange of letters, written around 112, between the Emperor Trajan and a provincial governor named Pliny.[2] Pliny acknowledged that there had been trials of Christians in the past, but he had never been present for one. Thus, he admitted, he was "unacquainted with the method and limits to be observed either in examining or punishing them." Again, it was assumed that Christians were routinely tried in court *for being Christian*; and, when they were found guilty, they were punished.

Pliny wanted to proceed cautiously. So, he explained,

> I interrogated them as to whether they were Christians; if they confessed it I repeated the question twice again, adding the threat of capital punishment; if they still persevered, I ordered them to be executed. For, whatever the nature of their creed might be, I could at least feel no doubt that defiance and inflexible obstinacy deserved chastisement.

Again, the governor—even at his most cautious—

---

[2] Pliny the Younger, *Letters* 10.96.

assumed that Christianity was not only a crime, but a crime worthy of death. He admitted that he understood little of "their creed," but he knew it to be criminal.

He went on to describe how he put everyone denounced as a Christian to the test. He ordered them to curse Christ and make an offering of wine and incense to the Roman gods. Anyone who complied went free. Anyone who refused was put to death.

The emperor responded that Pliny's method was "extremely proper." The governor had apparently done well.

Again, it seems that the trial and execution of Christians was not all that unusual. It was uncommon enough that a prominent lawyer like Pliny might rise in his profession without handling such a case. But such persecution was common enough that Pliny should be embarrassed for his lack of experience and feel the need to consult with his superior.

That was the situation of Christians in the empire through much of the Roman era. Persecution was always possible and it was often a threat, but it was only occasionally bloody and widespread. Most of the time, persecution took the form of a constant prejudice, disfavor, and exclusion from trades and social position.

Sometimes a husband who tired of his wife would denounce her as a Christian so that she would be killed and he would be absolved from paying her support or returning her dowry.

Sometimes a businessman would denounce his competitor as a Christian in order to eliminate competition.

When the law was convenient, it was enforced. And that

took place often enough for Christians to live in habitual expectation of persecution, even to death.

I don't want to give the impression that the Roman Empire ran as a round-the-clock slaughterhouse for Christian martyrs. That wasn't the case. Blood persecution was intermittent, sporadic, and sometimes geographically scattered. There were occasional massacres and purges, but only a few instances of systematic bloodletting. Some of those, however, were epic in scale.

⚜

In the Introduction we discussed Nero's persecution. The Roman historian Tacitus reported that an "immense multitude" perished in Nero's grand spectacle in July of 64. We do not know if his persecution extended beyond this single episode.

There are reports of other, smaller incidents in the decades after Nero—and even the decades before. The next major outbreak, however, likely came in the last decade of the first century, under the Emperor Domitian.[3] The letter of Saint Clement to the Corinthians and the Bible's Book of Revelation are notoriously difficult to place on a timeline; but both seem to refer (cryptically) to some tribulation visited upon Christians by Rome. Later historians, Hegesippus (second century) and Eusebius (third–fourth century), state that Domitian instigated a persecution and that it focused especially on Chris-

---

[3] For a detailed discussion of the evidence for Domitian's persecution, see Marta Sordi, *The Christians and the Roman Empire* (Norman, OK: University of Oklahoma, 1994), 43–53.

tians who were members of noble families. Domitian may have set in motion the program of persecution that eventually claimed Saint Ignatius—and the victims of Pliny.

Continuing through the second century, there were flare-ups in the provinces and instances of mob violence. But as the Church grew, persecution became a more unwieldy task. Particular Christians were, moreover, extremely valuable in their professions. Was it worth the trouble for the Romans to prosecute Christian soldiers, for example, and thereby weaken and demoralize the military? The answer to that question differed at various times in the empire's history. During the late second century, accommodation of Christians rose to new heights. During the reign of Marcus Aurelius (161–180) there was an all-Christian unit, the Thundering Legion, who were prized for their valor—and the help they received from their God.

But as the Christians' fortunes rose, so did occasions for envy and suspicion. During the years of the Severan emperors, as the second century turned over to the third, the authorities decided once again to crack down. At this point, the Christian Church had grown so large that an all-out persecution would have been catastrophic for both the persecutors and the persecuted. So the Roman authorities tried instead to contain the problem by forbidding *conversion* to Christianity. It was this round that claimed adult catechumens such as Saints Felicity and Perpetua, whose prison diary remains a classic of Christian literature. The Severan persecution seems to have been most intense in North Africa.

In the 230s the Emperor Maximinus Thrax tried a different approach. He targeted the clergy, including the pope and other prominent theologians. None of these seemed to work. One of the great Christian writers of the era, Tertullian of Carthage wrote: "The more you mow us down, the more we grow in number. The blood of Christians is seed."[4]

Tertullian's phrase became something of a rallying cry, and it is still paraphrased today: *The blood of the martyrs is the seed of the Church.*

That seed would be sown widely as the third century wore on. The Emperor Decius, in the year 250, issued an edict requiring a religious test for all inhabitants of the empire. Everyone would have to offer sacrifice to the gods of the Roman pantheon, and the act of sacrifice would be recorded on a certificate (Latin, *libellus*). This certificate had to be shown on demand as proof of one's loyalty to Rome and rejection of Christian principles. Some bishops lamented that crowds from their congregations rushed to offer sacrifice and save their lives. Yet many Christians chose to die rather than worship idols. In Carthage, North Africa, and Alexandria, Egypt, the persecution raged ferociously, and it is likely that thousands of Christians were killed.

The program begun by Decius was far more systematic and thoroughgoing than those of his predecessors. It was renewed and sustained under his successors Valerian and Gallienus, thus lasting for more than a decade.

By far the most extensive persecution, however, was that of Diocletian. It is often called the Great Persecution, and it

---

4 Tertullian, *Apologeticum* 50.13.

was indeed ruthless. Diocletian began his reign in 284. Never fond of Christians, he began by eliminating them from positions of military and governmental leadership. His co-leader Galerius pressed him to go still further in suppressing Christianity, and these urgings were confirmed in 302 by an oracle purported to come from the god Apollo. Eager to comply, Diocletian issued a series of edicts that stripped Christians of their civil rights and required them to conform to traditional (pagan) religious practices. The Great Persecution proceeded with a "grim thoroughness"[5] and continued until 313, when the Emperor Constantine issued a series of edicts guaranteeing religious toleration throughout the empire.

We don't know how many Christians were killed in the Great Persecution or in the earlier periods of trial for the Church. It's likely that we'll never know. Estimates range from tens of thousands to hundreds of thousands.

They were many, and yet their testimony led to the conversions of many more. Around 150 Saint Justin said that his own embrace of Christianity began when he saw martyrs courageously facing death. Through the centuries of persecution—from 50 to 313—the Church grew at a steady rate of 40 percent per decade.[6]

The hostile empire proved to be fertile ground for the Gospel—and, yes, the blood of the martyrs was seed.

---

[5] D. Vincent Twomey and Mark Humphries, eds., *The Great Persecution: The Proceedings of the Fifth Patristic Conference*, Maynooth, 2003 (Dublin: Four Courts, 2009), 7.

[6] See the sociological analysis of Rodney Stark in his books *The Rise of Christianity* (San Francisco: Harper, 1997) and *Cities of God* (San Francisco: Harper, 2006).

The martyrs emerged as the great heroes of the early Church. The historian-bishop Eusebius said that Christians everywhere depended upon the intercession of the martyrs.[7] Their death was seen as a participation in Christ's passion— atoning, like Jesus' death, for the sins of others. They shared Saint Paul's deep conviction: "Now I rejoice in my sufferings for your sake, and in my flesh I complete what is lacking in Christ's afflictions for the sake of his body, that is, the Church" (Colossians 1:24).

Popular devotion to the martyrs gave rise to new genres in literature. The "Acts" of individual martyrs began from court transcripts of interrogations, which were then supplemented with eyewitness descriptions of the martyr's suffering. The earliest example that has survived is *The Martyrdom of Polycarp*, and it is the first text to use the words *martyria* and *martys* unambiguously in their technical Christian sense.

A second related literary genre was the "exhortation" addressed to those who were facing martyrdom, urging them to remain steadfast and faithful through all the threats and tortures to come.

Tertullian wrote his *Ad Martyras* at the outset of the Severan persecution in 197. Tertullian would eventually win renown as the first eminent theologian writing in Latin. A convert to Christianity, he was already an accomplished law-

---

[7] See the introduction to his work *The Martyrs of Palestine.*

yer and rhetorician. *Ad Martyras* was the first major work he produced as a Christian.

In its pages we see how the Christian Church was united in mutual support. Everyone did what he could. The martyrs made their witness as they awaited execution in prison. Their fellow Catholics brought them food and tried to supply whatever comforts they lacked in their cells. Since others were supplying the bodily wants, Tertullian offered something for the soul. "For it is not well for the body to be filled and for the spirit to hunger." He exhorted them not to slacken in their spiritual disciplines as the day of their death approached. He reminded them that their task was nothing less than warfare—spiritual warfare. They had been called to do battle, not with the gladiators or the beasts, who would undoubtedly "win" in the struggle for bodily life. No, they were contending visibly in spiritual warfare that would be the culmination of their Christian life: "We have been called to the military service of the living God since the moment when we responded to the words of the Sacrament."

For Tertullian—and for all the authors of martyr-related literature—Christians were called to battle with Satan. In ordinary life, this took place invisibly, in the heart, the mind, the conscience. When, however, persecutors commanded or invited Christians to worship idols, the warfare was no longer invisible. It was brought out into the open, for everyone to see. It was a public testimony to the strength of Christ, who was alive in the Christian.

He didn't gloss over the hardships. He acknowledged the

foul conditions of the prisons where they were held. He spoke plainly about the difficulties ahead of them. He wanted them to be prepared, and the best way to prepare them was by plain speaking, not euphemism or evasion. All of their privations were merely the normal conditions of troops during wartime: "No soldier goes to a war equipped with luxuries, nor does he go forth to the battle line from his bedroom, but from light and narrow tents wherein every hardship and roughness and discomfort is to be found."

Tertullian drew from Scripture. He reminded the prisoners of the bravery of pagan historical figures—men and women who had endured hardship and death for the sake of earthly glory, family honor, or other lesser motives. The Christian should be empowered to do far more for Christ. He assured them they would receive the grace sufficient for their moment of trial. If they corresponded to that grace faithfully, they would give testimony.

Almost half a century later, in Palestine, the great Egyptian scholar Origen wrote a much longer Exhortation to Martyrdom, addressed to two priests as they awaited the execution of their death sentence. Like Tertullian's address, Origen's essay is passionate. He treats martyrdom as the most perfect act of love. However, he wrote as a Scripture scholar, and so he presents much more detail from the Bible, both the Old Testament and the New, presenting examples of the courage men and women showed when called upon by God. Origen's own father had died as a martyr—and left his son with an abiding desire to become the same sort of hero and lover. Origen's

Exhortation is much longer than Tertullian's *Ad Martyras*, and a much richer work.

The martyrs represented a different sort of hero in the ancient world. Whereas the heroes of Greek and Roman epic were invariably male, many of the most beloved Christian martyrs were women: Perpetua and Felicity in Africa, Blandina in Gaul (France), and Agnes in Rome. And, while the heroes of pagan epic were usually warriors—whose value rose with their body count—the Christian heroes were victims. The martyrs were losers in the eyes of the world, but winners in the divine economy. The task of those authors who exhorted the martyrs awaiting death was to take the invisible and make it vividly visible in the mind's eye—to make the prisoners keenly aware of the battle they face and the stakes to be won or lost.

⚜

The literature of martyrdom is abundant from the early centuries, and so is the material culture. We have already mentioned reliquaries and churches built to contain the relics of the martyrs. We should also mention the catacombs, the network of burial tunnels built underground on the outskirts of Rome. Many inscriptions in the Roman catacombs memorialize the martyrs who were buried there. Much of the graffiti on the walls—some of it dating back to the third century— begs the martyrs for their intercession.

The martyrs made a lasting impression on all those who

saw them suffer. Christians went home fortified for their daily struggle of living in a hostile culture rife with violence, injustice, and sexual immorality. By the early second century, the Christians were already renowned for their courage. They took up disciplines of prayer and fasting in order to prepare themselves in case they were called upon to die for the Faith. The pagan philosopher Epictetus observed that madmen came to fearlessness by way of their illness, but Christians acquired fearlessness "by way of habit."[8]

The Romans could always find reasons to step up the persecution of Christians. It was a solution to social problems. Christians were "divisive" (see Matthew 10:34–36), and the authorities believed that punishment would eliminate the troublemakers and cow their survivors into submission. It didn't work.

Governors claimed, too, that Christians were responsible for any ills that plagued their cities. Tertullian mocked this attitude, which must have been common in his day: "If Tiber floods, and Nile does not; if the sky stands still and holds back its rain, if the earth quakes; if famine or pestilence take their marches through the country, the word is, 'Away with these Christians to the lion!' Bless me! What, so many people to one lion!"[9]

And, after the lion was well fed, the social problems remained.

The emperors needed to keep the people well fed, distracted, and amused. For this they provided circus spectacles

---

[8] Recorded in Arrian, *Discourses* 4.7.
[9] Tertullian, *Apologeticum* 40.

full of sex and violence. In the Christians they found a ready supply of victims. But, after a while, the people were no longer amused. It wasn't fun to watch people die bravely. In fact, the martyrs' virtue made spectators feel ashamed of their own shallowness and spiritual poverty.

While the Church celebrated the love of the martyrs, Christians daily prayed for peace. Though God would always be with them as they faced temptation and evil, still they asked (in the Lord's Prayer) to be delivered from both. Still, they worked to increase understanding and tolerance and to overcome anti-Christian bigotry and fear.

Most importantly, they continued to live faithful lives, which were lives full of charity. Tertullian noted that Christians were most famous for the indiscriminate kindness they showed to their neighbors. Christians lived lives of generosity, justice, and purity; and such a life made them happy. They had happy homes, and their pagan neighbors wanted, more and more, to have what the Christians had.

They could not get it by taking it away from the Christians. They tried that, and it didn't work. Gradually, they gained it by conversion. By the early fourth century, the Catholic Church represented the single largest religious body in the empire. The authorities knew the game was over. Even the holocaust perpetrated by Diocletian could not stop the effects of Christian witness.

In February 313 the Emperor Constantine declared an end to persecution. His Edict of Milan established, for the first time in history, a climate of religious tolerance. It was a cause for celebration, an occasion for forgiveness, but not for forgetting. The liberated Christian Church—and Constantine himself—emerged from the shadows and immediately built grand memorials to the martyrs of centuries past.

That memory would serve the Church well.

CHAPTER 5

Not to the Lions, But to the Margins: The Case of Julian the Apostate

Constantine's edict, in 313, arrived as an answer to prayers. Prominent Christian thinkers—like Eusebius—believed the "Peace of the Church" would now be permanent, the fulfillment of God's kingdom on earth. Christians would, at least in the Roman Empire, practice their faith freely and without fear.

It was not to be. In the years following the Peace, the Church was riven by a new and controversial movement in doctrine. It was named for Arius, the Egyptian priest who was its origin. Arius denied that Jesus was divine in the way God the Father was divine. He denied that the Son was coequal and coeternal with the Father. Thus, his teaching subverted the ancient Church's faith in the Trinity and the incarnation of the Son of God. Apart from these truths, salvation in Christ made little sense.

Arianism spread like a virus or a poisonous weed, and wherever it went it divided congregations and churches. Constantine grew concerned that this new idea could destroy the peace he had taken great risks to establish. He worried, too, that Arianism would cause disunity in the empire, as church-es and regions declared themselves for or against the doctrine of Arius.

He convened a council of the world's bishops—men on both sides of the question—so that they could peacefully set-tle the dispute. In 325 they met in Nicaea and they judged Arius to be badly mistaken. They declared him to be a her-etic and excommunicated him and anyone who followed his doctrine.

Yet Arianism persisted and spread all the more. Constan-tine's heirs were his sons, who were themselves divided on the question of Arianism. The matter became deeply politicized, as members of one faction or another were appointed as gov-ernors or bishops. Christians had not long before been perse-cuted. Now, some of them were persecuting others.

Brave bishops like Saint Athanasius suffered exile and were even sentenced to death. Their only crime was their de-fense of the apostolic faith.

Amid such instability, the rulers knew their positions were extremely insecure. Constantius II, who ruled the east-ern part of the empire, decided to eliminate any potential rivals. He murdered nine family members, including his fa-ther's half-brother and most of the man's children. Two small boys were spared. One of them was named Julian.

Now orphaned, Julian still lived a life of privilege as a member of the imperial family. He received an excellent edu-cation. He was raised, of course, to be a Christian.

Julian seethed with hatred for the family members who

killed his father. He hated everything about them, but most of all their hypocrisy. They professed to be pious, yet they killed their closest kin.

Still, Julian could not risk their disfavor. He bided his time, and he did as his cousin, the Emperor Constantius, wished him to do. He attended Mass and went through the motions of Christian faith, but he refused to believe in the religion of his murderous relations. Secretly he began to study the old, pagan ways.

Constantius appointed him to be a military ruler in Gaul (modern France); and Julian showed himself to be a canny, disciplined leader, inspiring the respect of his troops. On the battlefield and in camp, he claimed no special privileges because of his rank. He ate what his men ate and slept as they slept. He made sure they were paid well. And he won their loyalty.

Constantius died when Julian was thirty years old, and Julian found himself sole ruler of the entire empire. Now he had all the power his cousin had held. He had the army firmly behind him. He was accountable to no one on earth, and he no longer needed to pretend to be Christian.

He proclaimed that, as emperor, he was going to recover Rome's ancient values and save the empire from falling apart. Key to this restoration was to be a revival of the old religion. He ordered that the pagan temples—which had fallen into disuse and disrepair—be renovated and their priesthoods refurbished.

Through his actions he made it clear that he had no use

for Christianity—and, indeed, had contempt for the Church. He declared that worshippers of the old gods would be preferred for all civil service jobs. He began to receive visitors only in pagan sanctuaries, which were a horror to Christians. When Christians tried to complain, he ignored them. They had no access to him.

Since he had been raised a Christian, Julian knew well how to disrupt the churches and cause division. He encouraged all the bishops who were exiled during the Arian controversies to return to their sees. On the surface, that appeared to be an act of mercy, but he wasn't doing it to be nice. He wanted to renew divisions in the churches and thereby weaken the Faith. When the exiled bishops arrived, some of them placed themselves squarely in opposition to the seated bishop, who then returned the favor.

While dividing the Church, Julian sought to unite paganism as it had never before been united. There had never been one single pagan religion. The Roman gods were many, and each had temples and cults, but none of them demanded exclusive worship. People could choose as many or as few of them as they wished, and offer sacrifice whenever they felt the need.

Julian changed all that. He declared that Roman religion should be organized as a mirror image of the Christian church. He organized the priests into a hierarchy with the emperor as a sort of pope over it all. He took a keen interest in the discipline of the priests. He ordered the establishment of pagan charities for social welfare—for the first time in history. As he caused dissension among Christian clergymen, he took pains to strengthen their pagan counterparts.

Julian was careful not to do any of the things the Christians might associate with an old-fashioned Roman persecution. As a lapsed Catholic he knew well that "the blood of the martyrs is seed." He wanted to render the Church sterile, so he was careful not to spill blood.

Instead, he found ways to squeeze them out of public life. First he made the requirements for schoolteachers so stringently pagan that no Christian could fulfill them. Yet he insisted he was not excluding them from education. They could, after all, continue to run their Sunday schools. "If they want to learn literature," he said, "they have Luke and Mark: Let them go back to their churches and expound on them."[1]

Next he did the same thing with the legal profession. Then he forbade Christians to hold funeral liturgies during the day.

Against the Church he was obstructionist, passive-aggressive, and disingenuous, but always calculating, calm, nonviolent. He wanted to move Christians to the edges of public life—and then push them out entirely. He called them "Galileans," emphasizing their provincial origins. He called Jesus "the Nazarene" for the same reason. He implied that Christianity might exercise influence in its original backwater villages, but it had no business operating in the imperial capital.

Julian, meanwhile, wrote a book whose title left no doubt about its purpose: *Against the Galileans*. It is a deriva-

---

[1] Quoted in Peter Brown, *The World of Late Antiquity: AD 150–750* (New York: W.W. Norton, 1989), 93.

tive work, drawing from anti-Christian tracts of the second and third centuries. (The work of the so-called "New Atheists" in our time does little more than rehash these ancient arguments.)

Yet, again, he never ordered bloodshed. He didn't need to. He had created a climate of contempt for Christianity. People could read between the lines of his laws and his pamphlets. The emperor, moreover, was young and strong, and he would probably occupy the throne for decades. Those who wanted to advance their careers were eager to make a show of their sympathy for his cause.

Then Christians began to die—not at the hands of governors, but rather at the hands of a mob. In Lebanon, a bishop and a deacon were lynched. Similar incidents erupted in Asia Minor, Egypt, and Palestine.

Julian could not officially approve such actions, so he praised them with faint damns: "Though I wish to praise you, I cannot, because you have broken the law. Your people dared to tear a human being in pieces as dogs tear a wolf."[2] He conceded that the victims probably deserved what they got—nevertheless, the law must be observed. In the end, the mob got a slap on the wrist and two pats on the back.

Julian wished to neutralize Christian influence in Roman culture and society. What he could not accomplish through the law, thugs would accomplish outside the law. He made all the right moves. He was certain he would win.

---

[2] Quoted in Adrian Murdoch, *The Last Pagan: Julian the Apostate and the Death of the Ancient World* (Rochester, VT: Inner Traditions), 137.

But he didn't. He had reigned less than three years when the Persian military began to advance on the eastern borders of the empire. Julian led his army to meet them in battle, and he was brought down by a spear. According to the ancient histories, his dying words were: "You win, Galilean."

How strange that the world had moved on from Roman religion—even Julian's revised version—yet not from the persecution of Christians. A respite came, however, as Christian emperors succeeded Julian in office.

Nevertheless, Julian made his mark. Future despots would learn from his example how to marginalize Christians without killing them outright. They could leave the violence to the mobs.

Chapter 6

Death and Dhimmitude:
The Aftermath of the Arab Invasion

As the Roman world became Christian, the empire split increasingly into two functionally separate—but closely allied—halves, East and West. This was necessary for many reasons. The Empire had grown too large to be managed as a unit. The culture and customs in Syria and North Africa were vastly different from those in Britain and Gaul. The borders at one end of the Empire were threatened by different kinds of enemies from those at the other end.

Historians now describe the Eastern realm as the Byzantine Empire, because its capital was the city of Byzantium, also known as Constantinople. But in the first millennium both halves considered themselves to be simply "Rome"—heir to the most sprawling and most prosperous empire in history.

Its enemies grew stronger and more numerous. Tribes in the hinterlands began to organize and form armies, making incursions that reached even to the imperial capitals. Rome's great enemy to the East remained the Persian Empire, ruled by the Sassanid dynasty, which was ever eager to gain Rome's trade centers and ports near imperial borders.

The Roman Empire—East and West—was predominantly Christian by the end of the fifth century. The Persian Empire was officially Zoroastrian, but its lands were home to large Christian and Jewish minorities. Some of these, especially those who lived near the borders, were looked upon with suspicion—as interlopers or Roman spies, exiles who secretly hoped for a Roman rescue. So the persecution of Christians continued intermittently, though now on the other side of the ancient world. Under the Sassanids as under the earlier Romans, the crackdowns on Christianity were brief but intense, giving way to longer periods of toleration.

It is no doubt true that some Christians in Persian lands longed to enjoy the security and stability they imagined would come with Christian rulers. But it is a fact that many preferred to live beyond the reach of Byzantium, whose emperors, though Christian, could be heavy-handed in enforcing their will on the outlying provinces. Byzantine rulers were, unfortunately, as suspicious as the Persians about the Christians who lived in the borderlands—who read the Bible and celebrated the liturgy using the languages of Rome's enemy.

Such suspicion and bigotry led to divisions in the Church, some based on doctrine, but others based on region and culture. The Persians sometimes encouraged dissident Christian groups and offered them refuge. The divisions opposed one another fiercely. Emperors, keen to impose unity on their peoples, sometimes used violence to wipe out differences among Christians.

The results were not good. "Official" Christianity was too often marked by a servile and cynical complacency. Christians of one region, or one faction, cared little about the sufferings of Christians elsewhere.

These judgments sound harsh, and they are, but they are not mine. They were rendered in the seventh and eighth centuries by Christians[1] trying to understand the catastrophe of their time—the all-but-disappearance of Christianity from the lands where the Faith began and where the Faith had prospered, the lands we today call the Middle East.

At the beginning of the seventh century, the Sassanids were enjoying their second "Golden Era," having made alliances with many smaller neighboring nations. They pressed into Byzantine territory with renewed vigor, taking major cities such as Jerusalem and Alexandria.

While the Byzantines applied all their resources to resisting the Persians, they had to ignore the reports that were coming from the Arabian Peninsula, an area dominated by nomadic tribes. There, a man had succeeded in uniting many warriors who would in turn take up a religiously motivated war of conquest. His name was Muhammad. His authority, he said, came from the one true God, who wished all peoples to submit. Muhammad, in the course of his lifetime, won

---

[1] See, for example, John bar Penkaye, *Summary of World History (Rish melle)*, Book 15. An English translation is available at www.tertullian.org.

many people over. Most of the tribes in the Arabian Peninsula were polytheistic; they had worshipped many gods, and they made up the largest portion of his converts.

Muhammad was astonishingly successful. He took many towns and oases, and he absorbed many tribes, sometimes through battles, but sometimes without any resistance at all. The key to many victories was the ferocity of Muhammad's warriors, who had no fear of death. Indeed, they seemed to welcome it, as Muhammad had applied a traditional honorific term to his warriors who died in battle. It was a Christian term, martyr (*shahid* in Arabic), and it acquired a new meaning in the emerging religion known as Islam, whose followers were known as Muslims.

The text that Muslims hold sacred, the Quran, uses the word to describe anyone who dies in Islamic wars of conquest. Any Muslim warrior slain in battle received the title and the promise of a reward in the afterlife.[2]

Thus Muslim armies pursued their battles as fearlessly and single-mindedly as the Christian martyrs entered the arena to face the lions. There is a key difference, however. The Christian martyrs laid down their own lives, but took no one else's. The Arab warriors took many lives, including those of many Christians and Jews.

In less than a century, Muhammad's successors led armies from the edge of Egypt through North Africa to the Atlantic Ocean. They crossed the Strait of Gibraltar, took Spain and penetrated what is now southern France. They

---

[2] See, for example, Quran 9.111, 22.58.

made short work of mighty Persia and proceeded to India and Pakistan. Damascus fell in 635, Jerusalem in 638, Alexandria in 641, Carthage in 643, and Cyprus in 649. By 750, more than half the Christians of the world were living under Muslim rule.

Muslim conquerors sought conversion of the conquered. Christians and Jews were given a choice: they could renounce their faith and submit to Islam; they could keep their faith and pay a heavy tax; or they could be killed.

It would be impossible to calculate the numbers of those who died during the Arab conquests rather than renounce their faith.[3] Some died in massacres that left no survivors to tell the story. Some died in the course of battles. Others died at the hands of hostile neighbors. They were many, and they often fell in large cohorts.

Such widespread slaughter of Christians came as a shock to the once-Roman world. Christians had thought themselves secure. Faith was something they once had held effortlessly. Now it could be retained only by heroic effort.

The Christians of the Middle East had looked to the "age of the martyrs" as ancient history. Now they had to make sense of a new "age of the martyrs." The martyrs killed in the Arab conquests were qualified as "new martyrs" or "neo-martyrs," and in the East they continue to bear that designation even today, even after a millennium and a half!

---

[3] The records from this period are well catalogued. See David Richard Thomas et al., eds., *Christian-Muslim Relations: A Bibliographical History (600–900)* (Leiden: Brill, 2009) and Stephanos Efthymiadis, ed., *Ashgate Research Companion to Byzantine Hagiography* (two volumes, Burlington, VT: 2011, 2014).

Christian authors, such as the Persian monk John bar Penkaye, held that God was now purifying a Church that had grown lax, corrupt, and comfort-seeking. In the century when the Arab invasions began, John wrote: "When [God] saw that there was no amendment, he raised a barbarian kingdom against us, a people who would not hear supplications, who knew no compromise, no peace, and disdained flattery."[4]

Alas, martyrdom did not end with the conversion of old Rome. It continues in every age. The Christians of the seventh, eighth, and ninth centuries learned this the hard way, as martyrdom came to men, women, and children in Egypt, Syria, Palestine, Arabia, and the lands of the former Persian empire, the lands we today associate with Iran, Iraq, and Turkey.

Those who made the supreme witness bestowed a certain strength upon the Christians who survived them—the Christians who remained to live as *dhimmis*, oppressed minorities in Muslim lands. Some commentators have called this martyrdom on the slow burn. Dhimmis were taxed into poverty and denied all avenues of advancement in society.

Yet they kept the Faith; and their children kept the Faith; and their grandchildren kept the Faith; and their descendants remain faithful to this day. They have welcomed God's puri-

[4] John bar Penkaye, *Summary of World History (Rish melle)*, Book 15. The English translation by Roger Pearse can be found at www.tertullian.org. A generation before John, Saint Sophronius of Jerusalem offered a similar analysis of seventh-century events, to which he was an eyewitness: "Saracens entered the holy city of Christ our Lord, Jerusalem, with the permission of God and in punishment for our negligence, which is considerable." Robert G. Hoyland, *Seeing Islam as Others Saw It: A Survey and Evaluation of Christian, Jewish and Zoroastrian Writings on Early Islam* (Princeton, NJ: Darwin Press, 1997), 63.

fying mercy and grown stronger. They still await their deliverance, and by sheer endurance they give testimony to faith in the Lord and Redeemer, Jesus Christ.

CHAPTER 7
The First Police State and the Martyrs It Made

A millennium would pass before western Christians would experience the kind of divisions the eastern churches had known since the fifth century. The divisions in Europe arose with the Protestant Reformation, which gained momentum from the emergence of European nation-states. Whereas in the past, European peoples had seen themselves as (more or less) united in the common project of Christendom—and against the recurring threat of militant Islam—in the late Middle Ages they began to identify themselves with their geographic region and native culture. There was a flourishing of vernacular literature and distinctive styles of art and architecture. There was also a growing rivalry between neighboring rulers for regional dominance.

These divisions acquired a religious character with the Protestant Reformation, which began with the publication of Martin Luther's *Ninety-Five Theses* in 1517. There is no doubt that the Church was in need of spiritual renewal. The Church is always in need of spiritual renewal. Many of Luther's proposals would be necessary elements in any program of reform.

Some, however, threatened to overturn long-settled doctrine that the Church considered to be part of the apostolic heritage—and therefore non-negotiable.[1]

Both Luther and his interlocutors among the bishops tended to argue past one another, foregoing subtlety for polemic—and then mass-producing their polemics with the aid of the newly invented printing press. Great and intelligent humanists such as Erasmus of Rotterdam and Thomas More in England spoke up for moderate and measured reform, but their voices were lost amid the shouting, which soon led into pitched battles, which were bloody and not metaphorical.

Luther gained allies among the German nobles, who stood to gain financially and territorially if their national church should separate itself from the authority and influence of the Catholic Church. Rome and the papacy had stood, till then, as the great unifier in Europe, maintaining peace on the continent and ensuring that all peoples fulfilled their obligations to one another. Apart from Rome's discipline, the German nobles could exercise military and economic power as they wished.

As Luther's break became decisive, other Reformers arose with far more radical religious ideas. Luther opposed these, but his principle of religious autonomy had taken hold. The rulers of neighboring regions identified themselves with varieties of Christianity that were markedly different and vehemently opposed to one another. Disaster seemed inevitable,

---

[1] For a discussion of the revolutionary nature of Luther's religious reform, see the study by Frank C. Senn, a Lutheran theologian, "Sacraments and Social History: Postmodern Practice," *Theology Today* (October 2001): 294.

as the Muslim Turks soon began to exploit Europe's divided and increasingly vulnerable condition.

Religious dissent was punished severely—by all sides—and treated as treason or sedition, because to oppose religious unity was to oppose national unity (or European unity).

⚜

The Catholic Church in England was comparatively healthy. As an island apart—and a fledgling constitutional monarchy—England had avoided some of the problems associated with ecclesiastical politics on the continent. In his magisterial study of the period, Eamon Duffy of Cambridge observed:

> [L]ate medieval Catholicism exerted an enormously strong, diverse, and vigorous hold over the imagination and the loyalty of the people up to the very moment of Reformation. Traditional religion had about it no particular marks of exhaustion or decay, and indeed in a whole host of ways, from the multiplication of vernacular religious books to adaptations within the national and regional cult of the saints, was showing itself well able to meet needs and new conditions.[2]

---

[2] Eamon Duffy, *The Stripping of the Altars: Traditional Religion in England 1400–1580* (New Haven, CT: Yale, 1992), 4. For historical background on this period, see also Vincent Nichols, *Saint John Fisher: Bishop and Theologian in Reformation and Controversy* (Stoke-on-Trent: Alive, 2011).

England's king shared his people's religious solidity and traditional sensibilities. He himself authored a book defending the seven sacraments against the attacks of the Protestant reformers. For this effort he won notice from the pope, who declared him *Defensor Fidei* (Defender of the Faith). To this day, that title or its abbreviation, DF, has appeared on British coins alongside the image of the current monarch.

Henry was a man of above-average gifts. In addition to his amateur theological works, he wrote pleasant music and passable poetry. He was also a man of wild moods and appetites, indulgent to extremes of gluttony and sensuality.

Henry succeeded to the throne upon the death of his brother Arthur. He sought also to take Arthur's wife, Catherine of Aragon, as his own wife—as this would secure England's alliance with Spain, whose power was in ascendancy. Although Arthur and Catherine had been rightfully and legally married, they had never lived together or consummated their marriage. Henry petitioned Rome successfully for a dispensation from Church law, giving him permission to marry his brother's wife. It was granted.

And there the troubles began. Henry and Catherine consummated their marriage (and so sealed the alliance between England and Spain), but their union failed to produce an heir for the throne. Catherine suffered multiple stillbirths and the early deaths of two children, just a few days after birth. From Catherine's six pregnancies, only one child, Mary, would survive to adulthood. Henry grew anxious and despaired of Catherine's ability to bear a son.

He blamed the irregularity of their marriage, and interpreted their failure as divine retribution. He made another petition to Rome, this time to annul his marriage. He asked the current pope to rule that his predecessor had erred in granting permission for the marriage. The pope refused.

Henry was determined, and so he put the question to a number of prominent theologians. The case dragged on as the theologians disagreed with one another.

Henry chose to act anyway. He would hear no argument that countered his own. He would put away Catherine and marry Anne Boleyn, the aristocratic mistress he had already chosen to be his new wife.

Parliament confirmed Henry's divorce, and the pope drew up a bull of excommunication. The king responded swiftly with his Act of Supremacy, a law appointing himself and his successors as "Supreme Head of the Church and the Clergy of England."

This action placed Henry squarely on the side of the continental reformers. He would have denied that charge, because he tried to preserve (at least at first) the outward forms of traditional Catholic faith. But he, like Luther and the others, had violated the unity of the Church. The ancient tradition held that there was only one Church, spread throughout the world and found in all the different nations. The Church was one in doctrine and worship. It was universal, hence its name Catholic (from the Greek *katholikos*, meaning universal). Within the Church there were to be no distinctions between Jew and Greek, slave and free, English and French; all were Christians who shared one communion in one bread (see 1 Corinthians 10:17), and so all were Catholic.

Henry did his part to shatter that unity. The pope pronounced this action heresy because of the doctrine involved, which touched on the nature of the Church of Christ. As Henry would soon see, other doctrines fell in turn, as they depended on the inner coherence of the Christian tradition.

The pope had felt many political pressures to indulge the king. In those heated years of the Reformation, the nations were peeling off into one camp or another, depending upon the wishes of their monarchs. England had been one of the most powerful lands to remain in the Catholic fold, and so Henry was an important ally. And yet the pope could not bring himself to rule against truth and permit an injustice.

To say that people were uneasy with Henry's actions would be an understatement. But Henry made resistance very difficult. With a series of revolutionary laws, he required all men in the realm to take an oath accepting the king's supremacy in religious matters. Those who refused would face the penalties for treason, a capital crime. And some did. Thomas More, Henry's chancellor, committed no crime other than his refusal to take the oath. He did not oppose Henry publicly. He did not wish to cause scandal or division: "I am the King's faithful servant," he told his interrogator, "I say no harm, I think no harm, but I wish everybody good. And if this is not enough to keep a man alive, in good faith, I have no desire to live."[3] Before the House of Lords, More testified that he had made his conscience known to no one.

But Henry was determined to force consciences, and so More's conviction and execution were a foregone conclusion. He was beheaded in July of 1535 following Bishop John Fisher of Rochester who had been slain on June 22nd. Both men have been canonized as saints in the Catholic Church, and they share that date as their common feast day. (Their witness is particularly poignant for me since June 22 is also the date of my installation as Archbishop of Washington.)

Other executions followed, many of them grisly, designed to instill terror in Henry's subjects. To emphasize that their crime was religious in nature, Henry's henchman ("Vice-Regent in Matters Relating to the Church"), Thomas Cromwell, ordered that all of the condemned monks be executed publicly while wearing their religious habit. An Augustinian named John Stone received a sentence usually reserved only for those who physically attacked the king. He was hanged, drawn, and quartered.

Dragged by a horse to the gallows, Father Stone was then hanged by the neck with chains until he was almost dead. Then, while still conscious, he was slowly cut into four pieces, which terminated his life. This became the state's preferred method to be used against priests.

---

[3] Quoted in Christopher Dawson, *The Dividing of Christendom* (New York: Sheed and Ward: 1965), 112.

Henry considered himself to be traditional and catholic; yet he accomplished something more radical than any of the other reformers. He had introduced a deadly virus into the practice of statecraft. The political philosopher Eric Voegelin referred to the England of Henry VIII as the first totalitarian state. Henry's project, Voegelin said, "was not simply an assertion of national independence, and it was considerably more than a 'break with Rome.' It entailed, indeed, the establishment of the first totalitarian government, foreshadowing the possibilities of a future when the creed promulgated by the government would have become anti-Christian." In forcing consciences as he did, Henry prepared the way for Nazism, communism, and other despotic rules yet to come.[4] His methods would make many martyrs down the years.

They would make many in his own lifetime, as his vices and his failure to produce a male heir drove him to increasingly desperate measures. Married six times, he had two of his wives executed. In need of money, he seized the properties that had for centuries belonged to monasteries and turned them over to his cronies and flatterers.

Henry grew obese with age and suffered some disease that left him with running sores on his body. His waning years were pain-wracked and perhaps guilt-wracked. His last words were, reportedly, "Monks! Monks! Monks!"—which probably referred to the men he had made martyrs for the sake of his desires.

---

[4] Eric Voegelin, *History of Political Ideas: Religion and the Rise of Modernity* (Columbia, MO: University of Missouri, 1998), 75.

What Henry began, his daughter Elizabeth continued during her longer reign. Among her many victims was John Nelson, a Jesuit priest, whose only crime was his refusal of the oath. Father Nelson was drawn on a hurdle for three miles, from the prison at Newgate to Tyburn, where he was hanged, disemboweled, and quartered. His execution was presented as public entertainment—again, to terrify the people.

This is how Henry and Elizabeth managed to suppress England's Catholic faith, which, as Eamon Duffy pointed out, was vigorous up to the time of the Reformation. They did it by terror. They did it by claiming ownership of individual consciences. It is likely that more than six hundred men and women died as martyrs for the Catholic faith in post-Reformation England. In the British Isles, the Faith would be persecuted and Roman Catholics marginalized for centuries to come.

They were, in a real sense, martyrs especially for the Catholic vision of love, marriage, and family life. For Henry introduced not only totalitarianism into the social world of Europe, but also the notion of easy divorce. As king he pronounced himself head of the Church of England, and then he proceeded to discard wives as they outlived their usefulness to him. He set a precedent. It was bad for women. It was disastrous for children, families, and the social order.

But his martyrs served as a greater and more heroic model—followed in time by those many who resisted later tyrants, from Robespierre and Hitler to Stalin and Mao.

More and Fisher, Stone and Nelson we revere as saints.

And Henry? And Cromwell? Despite some recent attempts at rehabilitation by revisionist novelists and television producers, reasonable people still judge them to be despots.

CHAPTER 8

The Martyrs of Secular "Enlightenment": The Example of the French Revolution

The aftermath of the Reformation was a widespread and long-lasting "war of religion," with factions fighting against factions, all of them claiming the name Christian.

It is more accurate to speak of wars of religion, as there were around a dozen discrete conflicts; but ordinary people experienced them as never-ending battles. Indeed, they came to bear ominous names like "The Eighty Years' War" and "The Thirty Years' War."

These weren't purely wars of religion. Religious motives were often mixed up with brazen grabs for power and money. Many thousands of people perished, some as casualties in battle and some by execution, and God knows that many of them died in testimony to the Faith. The wars of religion, like the Arab invasions, produced a humanly incalculable number of martyrs.

It is understandable that such bloody exploitation— sustained over more than a century—should make some people cynical about Christianity altogether. For some observers, the witness of the martyrs was overshadowed by the counter-witness of the persecutors, who also claimed to act in the name Jesus Christ.

There arose, then, a movement in philosophy that argued for the removal of religion from any entanglement with government. The movement, known as the Enlightenment, lasted through the seventeenth and eighteenth centuries, and is associated with authors such as Thomas Hobbes and John Locke in England and Jean Jacques Rousseau and Voltaire in France. These men varied in their approaches to the problem of religious conflict. They ranged in their own belief, from atheism and agnosticism to deism (belief in a creator god who is unconcerned with the conduct of the world). Some sought a simple separation of church and state. Others were actively anti-religious.

What united them all was their rejection of revealed religion—which, for all practical purposes, meant Christianity. The Yale historian of the Enlightenment Peter Gay characterized the movement as "the rise of modern paganism." He wrote:

[T]heirs was a paganism directed against their Christian inheritance and dependent upon the paganism of classical antiquity, but it was also a *modern* paganism, emancipated from classical thought as much as from Christian dogma. The ancients taught the philosophes the uses of criticism, but it was modern philosophers who taught them the possibilities of power.[1]

Many of the movement's leaders did not bother to hide their scorn for Christianity. Voltaire called Christian religion "the infamous thing" and typically ended his letters with the line "crush the infamy." He judged Christianity to be "assuredly the most ridiculous, the most absurd and the most bloody religion which has ever infected this world."[2] Looking back upon the wars of religion, he concluded: "It is characteristic of fanatics who read the holy scriptures to tell themselves: God killed, so I must kill."[3]

Voltaire's friend and sometime patron, King Frederick the Great of Prussia, spoke of the belief of his subjects as "Christian fables, which are canonized by their antiquity and the credulity of absurd and insipid people."[4]

As the Scottish philosopher David Hume lay dying, his physician asked him if he had any regrets. He replied that he had just one. He "thought he might say he had been very busily employed in making his countrymen wiser and particularly in delivering them from the Christian superstition, but that he had not yet completed that great work."[5]

Such ideas could be dismissed—and their injustice ex-

---

[1] Peter Gay, *The Enlightenment: The Rise of Modern Paganism* (New York: Vintage, 1966), xi.

[2] Richard Aldington, trans., *Letters of Voltaire and Frederick the Great* (New York: Brentano's, 1927), 285.

[3] Nicholas Cronk, *The Cambridge Companion to Voltaire* (New York: Cambridge University Press, 2009), 199.

[4] Richard Aldington, trans., *Letters,* 116.

[5] Peter Gay, *The Enlightenment,* 356.

cused as ignorance—if they did not have catastrophic political consequences. David Hume was content to work at persuading his neighbors, by plodding argument, to abandon their faith. Some of his followers, however, would grow impatient with persuasion and turn to force. The wars of religion had come to an end, but now they would give way to bloody wars *against* religion, and specifically against Christianity.

Beginning in the eighteenth century and continuing to our own day, revolutionaries have sought in various ways to realize the anti-religious dreams of the Enlightenment philosophers. It is interesting to note that their ideologies increasingly assumed the form of religions. Consciously or unconsciously, the children of the Enlightenment, as they sought to form a new culture, appropriated religious language, imagery, iconography, and eschatology. They declared feast days, enacted rituals, spoke in terms of deliverance and salvation, and lifted up as idols Reason, the Individual, or the People—usually depicted allegorically in almost sacral terms. Sometimes they identified certain writings as almost sacred.

In opposing religion, ideology proved inadequate. The revolutionaries seemed to require a counter-religion.

Nowhere was that as literally true as in the French Revolution. Begun in Paris in 1789, the seizure of the government began with a promise of "liberty, equality, and brotherhood," but by late 1793 had given way to a Reign of Terror.

When the Revolutionary government failed to win the popular support it wanted, it turned eagerly to killing everyone who seemed to be an enemy. Tens of thousands were executed by guillotine, and still more were lynched by mobs or score-settling neighbors.

The leaders of the Revolutionary government were fiercely anti-religious, and they had a particular hatred for the Catholic Church, which had opposed the Revolution from the beginning. Like King Henry VIII, they laid claim to all church lands and commandeered property from prominent Catholics. They evicted priests, monks, and nuns and ordered them to earn a living. In another move reminiscent of Henry, they required all clergy to swear primary loyalty to the state, not to God or the Church.

Those who refused were summarily condemned. On the Ile Madame, in the River Charente, almost a thousand priests were imprisoned in horrid conditions and slowly starved. Hunger and disease killed 254 of them. In October 1995, Pope John Paul II beatified many of them as martyrs. One of them, Father Jean-Baptiste Souzy, succeeded in organizing a disciplined spiritual life for his fellow prisoners. They found a way to live as a community, a Church.

The Carmelite nuns in the town of Compiègne were evicted from their enclosure and then arrested. Condemned by the Revolutionary Committee for Public Safety, these gentle sisters were brought to Paris for execution. A crowd gathered to cheer, but was struck dumb by the sight of the nuns who, one by one, renewed their vows and sang hymns before ascending the scaffold to the guillotine. The crowd dispersed in silence, ashamed.

The revolutionaries seized the great Cathedral of Notre Dame, in Paris, and repurposed it as a temple dedicated to the goddess Reason. On the altar, they enshrined a prostitute as the goddess's representative. On the Feast of Reason they desecrated the sanctuary with blasphemous rites.

The greatest resistance to the Revolution came from the devout people of the rural Vendée region. When the military came to draft new conscripts, the farmers rebelled. They would not have their sons fight for the cause of blasphemy. They were poorly armed, however, and no match for the army sent from Paris. More than a quarter of a million people were massacred—and the army made a spectacle of the slaughter. Men, women, and children were drowned together in groups, or burned alive, or otherwise tortured to death. Their bodies were mutilated, and the organs and limbs were sent off for scientific experiments.

The "Revolutionary" persecution of Christians in France continued until the rise of the Emperor Napoleon, who restored the Church's freedom, but retained its property in the custody of the state.

So much for the dream of peace in a secular state—for the illusion of a downtrodden people waiting to be liberated from religion.

Unfortunately, such dreams die hard; and the horrors of the French Revolution recurred, through the next two centuries, in secularist revolutions in Mexico, Russia, Spain, Germany, Turkey, and many smaller countries.

In 1993 the Nobel Prizewinner Alexander Solzhenitsyn visited France to honor the memory of the victims of the Revolution. An Orthodox Christian, Solzhenitsyn himself had been arrested as an enemy of the Soviet state and had spent many years of his adult life in Russian prison camps. He said he had, since boyhood, drawn inspiration from the courage of the Christians in Vendée. Yet it puzzled him that humanity would let the same disaster happen again, falling repeatedly for the same empty promises of secularists.

One might have thought that the experience of the French Revolution would have provided enough of a lesson for the rationalist builders of "the people's happiness" in Russia. But no, the events in Russia were grimmer yet, and incomparably more enormous in scale. Lenin's Communism and International Socialists studiously reenacted on the body of Russia many of the French revolution's cruelest methods—only they possessed a much greater and more systematic level of organizational control.[6]

Solzhenitsyn gave a powerful testimony on their behalf.

---

[6] The text of Solzhenitsyn's address at Vendée can be found at http://www.vendee-guide.co.uk/Memorial-de-la-Vendee-Alexander-Solzhenitsyn.htm.

The martyrs, however, awaited no vindication. The community of priests on the Ile Madam knew they were dying, but they were dying more happily than their tormentors were living.

From anti-religious philosophers the Revolutionaries had learned "the possibilities of power." For the secularist fanatics, Voltaire's "crush the infamy" was more than a metaphor.

Yet what is power in this world? It's fleeting. Think again of Henry VIII dying miserably and guilty in his bed. Think, too, of the first wave of French Revolutionaries, consumed with suspicion till they all turned on one another in a long, uncontrolled bloodletting.

Then think for a moment of the joy of the Carmelites of Compiègne, even as they lost everything they had in this world. They were to be just another lot of victims of the Terror of Maximilien Robespierre. They would be buried in a heap with 1,300 other men and women identified as enemies of the state.

Shortly before they were taken to the place of their execution, the sisters gathered together and made a collective act of consecration, offering their lives as a sacrifice for the sake of the Church in an age of suffering.

Their vindication came swiftly. Within ten days, Robespierre himself was led to the guillotine, victim of the inevitable coup, and the worst of the Terror was brought to an abrupt end.

And by the end of the nineteenth century France was known again as a place of Catholic faith and culture, producing saints such as John Vianney and Thérèse of Lisieux, exporting missionaries to build churches in far-off Asia, and emerging once more as a world center of sacred music and art. The monasteries arose again and became centers of learning in the fields of history, liturgy, and theology.

The blood of the martyrs, indeed, is seed.

CHAPTER 9
A Century of Slaughter

Pittsburgh, Pennsylvania, when I was born and raised there, was a bustling center of the steel industry. The mills drew their workers from a steady stream of immigrants, many of them from Eastern Europe. Fleeing first from poverty, and then from Nazism, and then from communism, they found refuge in the ethnic enclaves of our smoky city. They filled the pews of our parishes and built their own distinctive churches. Priests fled to Pittsburgh, too. I was ordained as a priest for the Diocese of Pittsburgh, and it was my privilege to count these men as brothers.

In Pittsburgh's pews there were men who had been imprisoned for their faith. I know of one man, from Ukraine, whose fingers were as gnarled as the limbs of an old oak. When he was young he suffered imprisonment for his Catholic faith, not once but twice, and the guards found many occasions to visit cruelty on him. Every one of his fingers had been broken at least once and left to set and heal without medical care. He survived; but he knew many others who did not.

The exiled Czech poet Rio Preisner also found a home in our diocese. Dr. Preisner had served time in prison under both the Nazis and the Communists before the latter finally expelled him in 1968. He told of how imprisoned Catholic priests—at great risk—would look for opportunities to gather a scrap of bread and a few drops of wine, so that they could celebrate Mass for their fellow prisoners. The "congregation" would create a human shield by pretending to read broadsheet communist newspapers. The priest then would offer the sacrifice in the shade of his persecutors' propaganda. Dr. Preisner told the story so that his fellow prisoners, and that courageous priest, would not be forgotten.

During the occasional "thaw" in Cold War relations, Catholics from the Eastern Bloc would come occasionally to visit family members in the Pittsburgh area. They would spend a week or two before returning home to their work, their risks, and the government's constant surveillance. One such visitor was Father Jerzy Popieluszko, a young Polish priest who was chaplain to the Solidarity labor union. Father Jerzy visited Pittsburgh in 1972, 1974, and 1976, staying with relatives in the suburbs and saying Mass at a city parish.

He preached insistently against the injustices of communism, and for his efforts he was regularly harassed, detained, and threatened. Eventually his travel was restricted. His Stateside cousins urged him to take refuge in Pittsburgh, as they themselves had done. While Father Jerzy respected those who fled, he knew that God wanted him to serve his people in Poland.

After 1976 he never made it back to our land. On October 19, 1984—just a month past his thirty-seventh birthday—he was kidnapped by three members of Poland's secret police. They beat him to death and threw his body into the Vistula River.

It is estimated that a million people turned out for his funeral Mass in Warsaw. It was a striking public witness of homage for a martyr—a triumph of faith over oppression. Historians believe that day was the beginning of the end for communism in Poland. Father Jerzy was beatified by the Church in 2010.

"Confessor" is the name the ancient Church applied to those who suffered for the Faith, but were not killed. The Romans, knowing the Christians' reverence for martyrdom, would sometimes deny them the privilege—torturing them so that they would live on in pain, or blindness, or incapacity. They did this, in the third century, to Origen of Alexandria, who wrote the famous *Exhortation to Martyrdom*.

The twentieth century, the century in which I lived most of my life, made millions of martyrs; and it made many, many more confessors for the Faith, men and women who lived to keep the memory of the great persecutions. They told the story with the words and with their wounds.

Make no mistake: the century past was a century of horrors visited upon Christians. Genocide is the term applied to the deliberate killing of a large ethnic group of people. The goal of genocide is extermination, the total elimination of a group of people who are identified as a threat. Such programs, directed against Christians, began early in the century. They have been most thoroughly documented by Dr. Robert Royal in his monumental study *The Catholic Martyrs of the Twentieth Century: A Comprehensive World History*.[1]

The Soviet dictator Joseph Stalin reportedly once said, "A single death is a tragedy; a million deaths is a statistic." The categories, of course, are not mutually exclusive. The statistics on twentieth-century Christian martyrdom are staggering. The demonstrable fact that such attempts at mass annihilation can happen again and again is truly tragic.

The Armenian Genocide. This was the event for which the word "genocide" was coined. Well over a million Christians were systematically exterminated by the Ottoman Turks in the years 1914–1918. It was a matter of state policy, overseen by a state organization in Muslim-ruled Turkey. Turkish inmates were freed from prison in order to serve as a paramilitary arm for the purpose of annihilating the country's Armenian minority, most of whom were Christians. These criminals enlisted the help of street gangs as they went about their work. Many Armenians were burned alive. Some were drowned; others were gassed or poisoned; still others were intentionally infected with typhoid fever. The worst of the atrocities took place in the year 1915, but massacres had occurred as far back as the 1890s, claiming thousands of victims, and they continued to erupt into the 1920s. The Armenian population plummeted during that period from around 1.7

---

[1] Robert Royal, *The Catholic Martyrs of the Twentieth Century: A Comprehensive World History* (New York: Crossroad, 2000).

million people to fewer than 300,000. (Since there were no reliable census records, these numbers are estimates.) Some sources place the body count much higher, perhaps as high as two million. The Turkish government has always denied its role in the atrocities, and has disputed the many eyewitness accounts of the massacres. As recently as 2015, when Pope Francis memorialized the Armenian victims, Turkey protested and recalled its ambassador to the Vatican. Pope Francis remained steadfast. He said it was his duty to honor the memory of the martyrs: "Concealing or denying evil is like allowing a wound to keep bleeding without bandaging it."[2] (In Washington, D.C., too, we marked the centenary that year, and it was my privilege to participate in the memorial.)

The Mexican Persecution. Anticlerical movements have waxed and waned in Mexico since the middle of the nineteenth century. An 1857 constitution banned religious education from the schools and prescribed the confiscation and sale of Church property. Such laws were irregularly enforced, because Mexico's government was unstable. The country's 1917 constitution, however, was still more hostile toward the Church, and its measures followed closely upon the policies of post-revolutionary France. It subordinated Church to state in most practical matters, while outlawing religious orders and requiring the closure of Church schools and seminaries. Priests were forbidden to wear clerical garb in public, and they received their ministerial assignments from the government.

---

[2] Pope Francis, Homily, Mass for the Faithful of the Armenian Rite, April 12, 2015.

Popular resistance escalated until the Cristero War broke out in 1926. Hundreds of clergymen were executed or lynched during this period. An estimated thirty thousand Catholic rebels (Cristeros) were killed. The most famous martyr of this period was certainly the Jesuit Father Miguel Pro. The atheist government made his execution (by firing squad) into a media event, hoping that news photos would frighten faithful Catholics. But instead the photos inspired the laity as well as his fellow clergy. Father Pro died courageously. As he faced the firing squad, he stretched his arms in imitation of Jesus on the cross. He shouted "Long live Christ the King!" as he was hit by a hail of bullets. The event was thoroughly documented and reported in the press. Though anticlerical violence largely ceased by the 1930s, the Church continued to operate under severe restrictions until the last decade of the century.

Soviet Communism. Karl Marx, the philosopher who first proposed modern communism, declared religion to be the great enemy of his proposed revolution. Religion, he said, "is the opiate of the people." In the first large-scale civil war to be based on Marx's ideas, the Russian Revolution, the greatest resistance came from Christian hierarchy, clergy, and devout laity. Vladimir Lenin, who emerged as the revolutionary leader, called such opponents "reactionaries" and ordered their execution. From its beginning the Soviet Union, while guaranteeing a right to belief, severely restricted the practice of religion—and actively punished any religious criticism of state policies or activities. Many Christians who suffered persecution by the Soviets were not arrested for explicitly "religious" reasons, but rather for crimes against the state. Bishops and clergy regularly vanished into labor camps, some of which were established especially for religious "criminals." As Soviet Russia sought to expand its sphere of influence, it typically shut down churches as completely as possible. In Ukraine, Czechoslovakia, Poland, and Romania, the Eastern Catholic Churches were officially liquidated and driven underground. Official Soviet records admit that hundreds of thousands of Christian clergy were executed as enemies of the state. The number of laity certainly numbers in the millions. It is likely that between fifteen and twenty million Christians died as martyrs under the Soviet Union. During a visit to Russia in 1931, Lady Nancy Astor, a longtime member of the British Parliament, asked the dictator Stalin: "How long are you going to continue killing people?" He replied: "As long as it is necessary."[3] And to Stalin—and to his successors—it often seemed to be necessary. Father Popieluszko was martyred in 1984, and he was not to be the last under Soviet rule. Once fearsome and apparently invincible, this officially atheistic empire began to crumble in 1989 and was dissolved within a couple years.

The Spanish Civil War. How is it that the most savage persecution of Catholics took place in a country where almost everyone had been baptized as Catholics? Most of the persecutors were lapsed Catholics, the neighbors and schoolmates of their victims. Spain's Civil War erupted in 1936, but it had been preceded by five years of unrest. The elected govern-

---

[3] Peter Juviler, *Freedom's Ordeal: The Struggle for Human Rights and Democracy in Post-Soviet States* (Philadelphia: University of Pennsylvania Press, 2010), 31.

ment, which was sympathetic to communism, turned a blind eye to violence and harassment directed against the Catholic Church. When a coalition of military generals rose up against the government, the government chose to arm its supporters among the general populace. The government swiftly enacted draconian anti-religious laws, and what followed was a long riot of bloodletting. In the first two weeks of the war, fifty priests were killed and many of the capital city's churches were ransacked. In the second month, more than two thousand priests and religious were murdered. By the time the war ended, after less than three years of fighting, thirteen bishops had been martyred, along with four thousand diocesan priests, and more than twenty-five hundred members of religious orders. One diocese in particular lost almost all its priests. "It is impossible to say exactly how many lay men and women were killed just because they were known as Catholics, but the number is quite large."[4] "People were arrested for as little as wearing a religious medal."[5] Amid such chaotic conditions, it was difficult to count casualties, but it seems that around half a million people were killed in Spain during the war, and many more went missing.

Nazi Germany. The German dictator Adolf Hitler hardly needs an introduction. He has become a symbol of evil, responsible for the near-extermination of Jews in Europe. He was also vehemently anti-Christian,[6] but shrewd

---

4   John Coverdale, *Uncommon Faith* (Princeton, NJ: Scepter, 2002), 186.
5   Robert Royal, *The Catholic Martyrs of the Twentieth Century*, 113.
6   For an account of Hitler's persecution of Catholics, see Ronald J. Rychlak, *Hitler, the War, and the Pope* (Huntington, IN: Our Sunday Visitor, 2010).

enough to keep this somewhat secret. Baptized Catholic, he had lapsed into a sort of nationalistic paganism. When in 1937 Pope Pius XI published an encyclical letter condemning Hitler's policies, the dictator launched a counter-attack against the Church. His efforts included unsuccessful plots to kill the pope. Other efforts were far more effective. He began to target outspoken clergy, especially in the lands he had conquered and occupied. No one knows exactly how many priests were killed, but the best estimate is that twenty-five hundred priests died in Nazi concentration camps, along with more than five hundred monks, about three hundred nuns, and six bishops. Many of the martyrs are now well known. The Franciscan Maximilian Kolbe died at Auschwitz after offering to die in place of another prisoner. Edith Stein (Sister Teresa Benedicta of the Cross) was a brilliant philosopher who also died at Auschwitz. Titus Brandsma was a Dutch religious brother and journalist who dared to oppose Hitler's policies against the Jews. Franz Jägerstätter was beheaded because he refused to serve in Hitler's military. Odoardo Focherini was an Italian journalist who helped Jews escape to safety; caught by the Nazis, he died in prison from medical neglect. All of these have been recognized as martyrs, beatified or canonized. Yet there were so many others. Some concentration camps had special barracks reserved for priests, who were especially ill-treated. In Poland, a predominantly Catholic country, millions of citizens were slaughtered.

Communist China. The People's Republic of China was established in 1949 after a long, bloody civil war. The communists who emerged victorious were led by a charismatic man, Mao Zedong, who was a brilliant propagandist, violent in his atheism. He wanted to destroy all memory of China's past and eliminate all foreign influences. And he placed Christianity in the latter category. During the Civil War, Mao encouraged anti-Christian violence after trumped-up "people's trials." Since nearly three-quarters of China's Christians were Catholics, the Catholic Church bore the brunt of his bigotry. Typical was the destruction of the Trappist Abbey of Our Lady of Consolation in 1947. Thirty-three monks were taken away and the abbey reduced to a smoldering ruin. The monks, some of them in their eighties, were stripped and forcibly marched from town to town. They were loaded up like pack mules and lashed and beaten as they went. Witnesses said that their flesh hung raw and bloody like meat. Most died along the way from the beatings or from exhaustion or dysentery. The hardiest men, the last six surviving through the march, were finally beaten to death, crushed with stones, or shot.[7] At the beginning of the Korean War in 1950, all missions were outlawed in China. Yet the Church endured. Mao tried to divert Catholic sympathies by establishing a national "Patriotic" Catholic Church and banning Roman Catholicism altogether. The Church has continued to operate underground and suffer persecution. Clergy and prominent lay people regularly disappear into detention, not to be seen for years. Yet the

---

[7] For details on these and other episodes, see Gerolamo Fazzini, *The Red Book of Chinese Martyrs* (San Francisco, CA: Ignatius Press, 2009) and Theresa Marie Moreau, *Blood of the Martyrs: Trappist Monks in Communist China* (Los Angeles, CA: Veritas Est Libertas, 2013).

Church has continued to grow. A recent demographic study concluded: "Is there a correlation between martyrdom and evangelization? In some countries we find that martyrdom was followed by church growth. A contemporary example is the church in China. In 1949 there were only one million Christians. Forty years of anti-religious communist rule produced some 1.2 million martyrs. The result: explosive church growth to today's 90 million believers."[8]

This chapter on the twentieth century could easily become a book of its own. But such a book, as I noted, has already been written. I have necessarily limited myself only to those persecutions that spilled over into Joseph Stalin's category of "statistics." But many more Christians perished in the twentieth century in many other corners of the world. Among the most famous was Bishop Oscar Romero of El Salvador.

Indeed, the most extensive statistical study indicates that there were forty-five million Christian martyrs in the twentieth century.[9] And the authors admit that their numbers are cautious and low, because they include only those who were "put to death," and not those who were left to die through secondary causes, such as disease or starvation.

The Church we know and love today is growing from the blood sown as seed in the last century. We should consider it our duty—a sweet obligation—to honor the memory of such recent martyrs.

---

[8] David B. Barrett and Todd M. Johnson, *World Christian Trends* (Pasadena, CA: William Carey Library, 2001), 231.

[9] See Barrett and Johnson, 228–237.

Chapter 10

The Amphitheater of YouTube: Martyrdom in Our Media Age

This chapter, I am sorry to say, must be written in real time.

The martyrdom I'm addressing is happening now—happening as I see these words appear on my computer screen. The same screen has shown me news—and offers to show me video footage—of the deaths of my fellow Christians in Iraq, Libya, Ethiopia, Syria, and elsewhere.

The videos are posted as a show of power. Defenseless men are beheaded on the seashore. Others are drowned slowly in a swimming pool as their tormentors film their struggle from below. Still others are locked in a vehicle that is then blown apart by explosives.

These most modern persecutors, like Nero so long ago, make a spectacle of their horrors. They hire professional videographers to edit the footage and set it to music.

A man who now lives in my archdiocese was for many years employed in the petroleum industry. A Catholic, he tried his best to get to Mass as he traveled in lands where any public display of Christian faith was severely punished. Mass times could not be advertised, so he was dependent on word of mouth. But executions were televised in that land, and he recalls when word went out among the Catholics to tune in and pray for one of their fellow parishioners whose sentence would be carried out the following Friday. The man, a Filipino expatriate, had made the Sign of the Cross in public and was charged with blasphemy. The standard punishment was to have his right hand cut off.

On television, the Catholics watched as the gentleman was given an opportunity to "repent" of his action. Instead, he made the Sign of the Cross—and that was the last time he used his right hand.

As we have seen in our glance at past history, it is often difficult to tally the casualties of a wave of persecution.

As we consider the martyrs who are our contemporaries, it is impossible to report accurate numbers because the numbers are constantly rising. We look to the Middle East and Nigeria and the Sudan and elsewhere, and we see people maimed, kidnapped, and killed by groups like the Islamic State and Boko Haram.

We receive a steady stream of information about atrocities inflicted on Christian women, children, and men in Iraq and Syria, and all of this cries out for a response. In August 2014, the patriarchs and Church leaders of the Eastern Churches met in Lebanon and denounced the "crimes against humanity" committed against their people. They condemned also the persecution and killing of other religious minorities, such as the Yezidis and Muslim sects.

It is difficult to measure the decline in Christian presence in the area; but in some places—in Iraq, for example—the Christian population has probably fallen by 90 percent over the last generation. A few decades ago, these Christians were a minority group, vulnerable, and living under pressure. Now their condition is far worse, as they have hardly any protection at all. The patriarchs lamented: "Christians in countries of the Middle East are suffering from harsh persecution, being kicked out from their homes and lands by extremists amid *total international silence*." (Emphasis added.)

Total international silence—this should be as unsettling for us as the range of horrors we see inflicted on those innocent men, women, and children. Do their lives matter? Apparently not—not to the news media, not to the diplomats, not to the heads of state who can rouse themselves to public displays of indignation in relatively trivial circumstances. Where is the outrage over these public tortures, carried out in the amphitheater of YouTube?

In the years after World War II, people in the United States gradually began to realize the extent of Nazi atrocities—the elimination of millions of people, the exploitation of millions more in labor camps, the subjection of live human beings to medical and scientific experimentation. We learned, in fact, that such crimes against humanity had been going on for years before our country entered the war.

Yet there had been no outcry. Indeed, refugees from those Nazi-occupied countries were turned away from our parts and sent back into the custody of their persecutors.

The disclosure went on for decades, and the sense of guilt and shame grew greater. Conscientious people cried, "Never again!" And they asked: Where was the outcry? How could such atrocities occur?

They occurred—and they continue to occur—for two reasons. Because there are those prepared to commit them and there are those who choose to remain silent.

The Nazis at least felt that they should hide their crimes away, behind barbed-wire fences, in gray, windowless buildings. Today's persecutors are proud of their actions. They brazenly make them public and even set the video footage to music, and they know they will suffer no repercussions.

In 2014, nearly three hundred schoolgirls, almost all of them Christian, were kidnapped by a jihadist group in Nigeria. The story occupied the networks for a news cycle and then vanished like a mist, though the girls were not recovered. Human-rights agencies received reports that some had been raped, enslaved, forced into marriages, forced to convert to Islam—but these reports were not considered newsworthy by the major media. Nor were they considered worthy of condemnation by leaders of nations.

When atrocities happen, there are many guilty parties. There are perpetrators, and there are those whom Thomas Merton called "guilty bystanders."

Read what Saint Paul said in the letter where he works out

his richest Eucharistic doctrine: "If one member suffers, all suffer together; if one member is honored, all rejoice together. Now you are the body of Christ and individually members of it" (1 Corinthians 12:26–27).

If we are taking Holy Communion and yet doing *nothing* to relieve the pain of our brothers and sisters whom we know are suffering, then are we not among those guilty bystanders?

Are we praying for them daily? This is the most pressing need. Are we praying that persecuted Christians will remain strong in the face of unimaginable pressures to abandon the Faith? Are we praying for particular people by name—prisoners of conscience whose stories we have come to know? Are we asking God also how, practically, we might do something to help?

Are we making our voices heard—writing to legislators and media? Where are the voices of parliaments and congresses? Where are the voices of campuses and business networks? Where are the voices of community leaders? Where are the voices of talk show hosts? Where are the voices on the nightly news? Where are the editorial columns and op-ed pieces expressing outrage? If all of these institutions heard an outcry from their Christian constituencies, they would perhaps be shamed into action. We live in a time when it is easier than ever to communicate with large numbers of people, whether through email, or social media, or the tried-and-true letter to the editor of the local newspaper. Each of us simply needs to use whatever forum available to make our voices heard.

Are we contributing financially to those organizations that are helping Christians in troubled lands? Agencies such as the

Catholic Near East Welfare Association, for example, and Catholic Relief Services are harboring refugees and advocating for those who bravely remain in their embattled neighborhoods. These are enormous undertakings that required daily infusions of funds. Unless we share what we have, our brothers and sisters will go hungry, and their children will have no medical care or access to education.

Are we seeking out these refugees in our cities and helping them to settle into a new home, new work, a renewed sense of dignity and Christian community?

Are we praying for the persecutors of Christians? Do we speak of them with charity even as we unflinchingly face their injustices? Do we desire their conversion to the Faith? Jesus commands us: "You have heard that it was said, 'You shall love your neighbor and hate your enemy.' But I say to you, Love your enemies and pray for those who persecute you" (Matthew 5:43–44). Remember that God gave the grace of conversion to the ancient Romans, who had made martyrs of the early Christians. God has won the hearts of countless persecutors throughout history, drawing them to the Church through the kindness of Christians. Jesus told us to pray for this earnestly, and he awaits our petition.

If we say we are Christian—if we say we are Catholic, which means *universal*—we are not free to ignore this great humanitarian crisis of our time. Sometimes, something falls so strongly on our conscience that we have to raise our voice. To be indifferent to the suffering and evil around us is to act in a way not worthy of our humanity, much less of our calling as Christians. History shows that the longer we fail to act against evil and aggression, the more difficult it becomes to eradicate the evil.

Let us act, so that no one may say we are complicit by silence in something so horrendous as the religious cleansing of nations.

Let us act, so that no one may say that we lack hope. Even in the face of these outrages, we believe in the power of prayer and we know that God's grace can touch and change every human heart.

Hearing the stories of Christian refugees who have been forced from their native lands—lands where Christians have been present since apostolic times—is indeed heartbreaking. But it is also profoundly inspiring. These sisters and brothers of ours fled with nothing but the clothes on their backs—and their Christian faith. They could have stayed simply by giving in, by becoming Muslim as demanded by their persecutors. But instead they gave up everything they had on earth, and they did it all for Christ.

You and I certainly face trials, troubles, and tests of our faith. We do face adversaries who want us to renounce or violate our principles. When we are put to the test of remaining firm in the Faith or giving in to the contrary demands of others, we should remember the witness of these modern-day martyrs. When we cry out to heaven, following their example, we will endure as they have endured, persevere as they have persevered, and will triumph as we know they will triumph at God's judgment.

☙

We live in a time of crisis for Christians who live in countries ruled by Muslim extremists. But I do not want to give the impression that these countries stand alone in persecuting Christians. Christians live with varying degrees of harassment and blood persecution in many different places. In some areas of Ukraine, Catholics suffer from harassment by imperialist Russians who wish to suppress or subordinate the Ukrainian churches that are in communion with the Holy See.

In India Christians face legal discrimination and mob violence, often orchestrated by Hindu nationalists, who dominate the political scene in certain regions. In 2008, Christians in Orissa were attacked by mobs. Some were killed. Religious sisters were sexually assaulted. Clergy were tortured in public. More than half of the one hundred thousand Christians in the city of Kandhamal were left homeless, their houses and businesses looted and burned as the people fled. Priests and their parishioners hid in the neighboring forests for weeks afterward, foraging for food and sleeping exposed to the elements.

In Mexico, priests and bishops have been martyred for daring to preach against the vile oppression of drug lords. In Sicily, priests have faced the same fate for preaching against the Mafia.[1]

Journalist John Allen describes the international situation vividly in the title of his recent book, *The Global War*

---

[1] Father Giuseppe Puglisi, a pastor in Palermo, counseled teens to excel in school and stay away from the mob. He preached against Mafia activity and died in a mob hit in 1993. The Church declared him blessed in 2013.

on Christians. He tells us that there is "a rising tide of legal oppression, social harassment, and direct physical violence, with Christians as its leading victims. However counterintuitive it may seem in light of popular stereotypes of Christianity as a powerful and sometimes oppressive social force, Christians today indisputably are the most persecuted religious body on the planet, and too often their new martyrs suffer in silence."[2]

Those who are suffering this way are Jesus Christ in our time. In them, he is walking the Way of the Cross.

And where are you and I? Are we Simon of Cyrene, ready to bear the burden for him—ready to bear the burden with them?

---

[2] John L. Allen, Jr., *The Global War on Christians: Dispatches from the Front Lines of Anti-Christian Persecution* (New York: Image, 2013), 1.

⚜

CHAPTER 11

Anti-Catholicism in America:
The Last Acceptable Prejudice

A few years ago I joined with hundreds of people gathered for an unusual event. We met at the reconstructed 1667 Brick Chapel in historic Saint Mary's City, Maryland, and we waited as the sheriff of Saint Mary's County unlocked its tall, sturdy wooden doors.

The sheriff used what seemed an oversized key. It was an exact replica of the key his long-ago predecessor had used to seal the chapel in 1704.

When the sheriff had done his part, I, together with representatives of the Jesuit community in Maryland, had the privilege of pushing open the doors.

The unlocking was a symbolic and ceremonial event, but it bore great significance for me and, I would say, for the city and land where I live. It was a reminder that we, in the United States, are a free people; and among the rights we celebrate are freedom of conscience and freedom of worship. But it also recalled that our own freedoms are fragile and easily compromised or lost.

In 1633, ships named *The Ark* and *The Dove* set sail from

England and after months at sea arrived in Chesapeake Bay. The passengers were nearly 150 brave women and men. They intended to establish the first American settlement to guarantee religious liberty to all inhabitants. The colony they built would become known as the birthplace of religious freedom in America: Maryland.

Unfortunately, by 1704 that generation of heroes had long since passed away; and political control of the land passed over to a less tolerant generation. In that year the colony revoked its former guarantees of religious freedom. Maryland's new leaders found it more convenient to silence the Church—by force—than to live in peace with her and her Gospel message. The Royal Governor ordered the Brick Chapel locked and never again used for religious purposes. The Jesuits later dismantled the chapel and used its bricks to construct a house nearby.

Despite this persecution, the Catholics in Maryland persevered; and eventually their freedom of religion was restored, enshrined as the "First Freedom" in the United States Constitution's Bill of Rights. Our nation's founders professed many different faiths. They were Catholic, Congregationalist, Deist, Episcopalian, Presbyterian, Quaker, and Unitarian. But they stood united for liberty.

Today, once again, people of good conscience must come together to stand for freedom of conscience and freedom of worship—for protection of religion from encroachment from the state.

I do not want to be misunderstood. I do not, in this chapter, intend to suggest an equivalency between the situation of Christians in America and the persecution of Christians in the Middle East. That would be untrue.

At the same time I do want to emphasize that freedom is a fragile thing. Rights, once lost, are not easily regained. And no land is safe from a sudden resurgence of persecution. Think about the bloodiest purges of the last century. Where did they take place? Catholic Spain. Orthodox Russia. Christian Germany. Christian Armenia. They began with small encroachments that grew greater over time.

To say "it can't happen here" is to speak from profound naiveté and ignorance of history.

In January 2012, Pope Benedict XVI warned the United States bishops of a "radical secularism which finds increasing expression in the political and cultural spheres" in our land. He went on to highlight his "particular concern" about "certain attempts being made to limit that most cherished of American freedoms, the freedom of religion. . . . The seriousness of these threats needs to be clearly appreciated at every level of ecclesial life."

How serious are these threats? Well, we live in a time when the Little Sisters of the Poor—a religious order dedicated to serving the neediest in our society—must appeal to the Supreme Court against the federal government's insistence that they commit actions that violate their conscience and their vows.

How serious are these threats? At George Washington University, a Catholic chaplain faced the threat of a "lockout" of his ministry simply because he had taught those who freely came to Mass what Jesus said about marriage.

How serious are these threats? Catholic medical students, interns, residents, doctors, and pharmacists increasingly face pressure to dispense "medicines" that induce sterility or kill human embryos.

The Church is denounced as prejudiced, narrow-minded, and even un-American simply because her teaching respects human life, upholds traditional marriage, and calls for health care for the most needy in our country. We hear, more and more, that our government cannot and will not tolerate such dissent. In places quite near to us—in Canada, in fact—Christians who promote traditional morality have been charged with hate speech.

When someone tells you, "You cannot speak here," the next sentence is often, "You do not belong here."

Our response must be the response of Jesus Christ, the response of his Church, a response rooted in love. We must continue to speak the truth, jealously guarding our rights, but prepared to face the consequences when people misunderstand us.

When others use force, there will always be a temptation to respond in kind. But we must respond as followers of Jesus Christ. We speak the truth in love.

The celebration we observed at historic Saint Mary's City was a tribute to the triumph of the human spirit over adversity and the ultimate victory of truth. But it was also a reminder that there are always those with a key, those who are ready to close us out of the public forum and our rightful and legitimate place in the debates that shape our society and our culture.

⚜

Philip Jenkins is a respected historian at Penn State and a prognosticator of religious trends worldwide. He identifies himself as an Episcopalian. He has written many bestselling books. In 2003 he wrote a shocking study called *The New Anti-Catholicism: The Last Acceptable Prejudice,* which he began with the words: "Catholics and Catholicism are at the receiving end of a great deal of startling vituperation in contemporary America, although generally those responsible never think of themselves as bigots."[1] Afterward, in page after page, he documented clear examples of "hate speech" directed at the Catholic faith and the Church's leaders—charges clearly libelous and delivered in language that no respectable person would use to describe any ethnic or racial group (or indeed any other religious community).

Jenkins argues that anti-Catholicism in America is comparable to anti-Semitism in other places at key moments in history. "Yet, while anti-Semitism is all but universally condemned, anti-Catholicism is widely tolerated."[2]

---

[1] Philip Jenkins, *The New Anti-Catholicism: The Last Acceptable Prejudice* (New York: Oxford University Press, 2003), 1.

[2] Jenkins, *The New Anti-Catholicism*, 5.

Jenkins' research speaks for itself, and in the dozen years since he published his book the situation has grown undeniably worse. I do not want to belabor the point.

But we Catholics, as well as other Christians, need to learn to decode the language of bigotry. We must also be prepared to speak up when cultural elites—in government, in academia, and in business—try to silence us. Over the course of a century, governments have made it increasingly more difficult for religious groups to operate schools, hospitals, and other institutions without violating conscience. This did not occur overnight. It happened because one law was built upon another, and then another law used that later law as a precedent, and then still another law came along. And we did not bother to speak up for ourselves. Instead, far too often, we chose to pay the tax, check the box on the form, and give up one after another form of our charitable work.

We have certainly surrendered far too much already; and with every surrender many other people have suffered—the people we serve, the people who depend upon us, the people who are vulnerable without the Church's ministry.

Since we have already lost so much, we have made it more difficult to protect what remains. Nevertheless, we must.

To identify with the martyrs does *not* mean we should roll over and die, so that our persecutors can walk over us.

The martyrs died fighting—not with swords or guns or other weapons, but with weapons of the spirit. They spoke the two-edged sword of the Word of God and shamed their captors and tormentors. They presented the face of

Jesus Christ to the world to the very end. They made sure that their protest was on the record. Their interrogation was in the books. You can still read it all in the Acts of the Martyrs.

If we would be faithful to their legacy, we must do the same.

Writing about the Roman martyrs, the fourth-century biblical scholar Saint Jerome said: "Let's not think that there is martyrdom only in the shedding of blood. There is *always* martyrdom."[3]

We are called to witness. We may endure denial, dismissal, and disdain. We can be disinvited and disinherited. We might become victims of political expedience in government, the corporation, and the professions. Our complaints are already mocked as "whining," self-pity, and melodrama.

Still we must be steadfast. We simply need to stand—to stand up for what is right, to stand up for what is ours, to stand up for freedom of religion. This is our heritage and our birthright.

> Consider him who endured from sinners such hostil-
> ity against himself, so that you may not grow weary
> or fainthearted. In your struggle against sin you have
> not yet resisted to the point of shedding your blood.
> (Hebrews 12:3–4)

---

[3] Saint Jerome, *De Persecutione Christianorum*, quoted in Boniface Ramsey, *Beginning to Read the Fathers* (Mahwah, NJ: Paulist, 1985), 133.

Not yet.

The author of the Letter to the Hebrews—who enjoyed the charism of divine inspiration—implies that many of his Christian readers will, however, have to face the test.

History has borne him out and proven him true.

CHAPTER 12
Martyrdom and the Eucharist

There is no user manual for martyrdom. Persecution is a test, but it's not the kind of test for which anyone can study in a textbook.

Even if there were such a book, many of the martyrs would not have been able to read it. In the time of the Roman persecutions, literacy was rare; there was no printing press; and Christian books were banned by law.

The martyrs followed no fixed set of rules as they gave their lives for Christ. Yet it is striking how similarly they speak in their final testimonies, and how so many of them fall into the same pattern of preparation for the end.

It is no surprise that they find a model in the Passion of Christ. He was falsely accused and unjustly tried. He was horrifically tortured and publicly humiliated. He was abandoned by his friends and left defenseless. Many of the martyrs mention points of correspondence between their ordeal and his.

There is a theme, however, that is more common in their testimonies. It is the Eucharist.

As the Eucharist is a re-presentation of Jesus' Passion, so is martyrdom. As the Eucharist is a voluntary self-offering, so is martyrdom. As the Eucharist brings about communion with Christ, so does the act of martyrdom. As the Eucharist is given so that others might live, so are the lives of the martyrs.

We see this pattern as early as the New Testament. Jesus speaks of his suffering as a chalice, a "cup," when he asks his Apostles if they are ready to suffer: "Are you able to drink the cup that I drink?" (Mark 10:38). Again, in the Garden of Gethsemane, as Jesus prays in agony, he speaks of his Passion as a cup: "My Father, if it be possible, let this cup pass from me" (Matthew 26:39).

Jesus identifies his own approaching martyrdom with a ritual act; and his action at the Last Supper leaves no doubt about which ritual act he meant. "And he took a cup, and when he had given thanks he gave it to them, saying, 'Drink of it, all of you; for this is my blood of the covenant, which is poured out for many for the forgiveness of sins'" (Matthew 26:27–28).

In the first Christian generation, the Apostles saw their own suffering as a sharing in Jesus' "cup." Saint Paul told the Philippians that he himself would be "poured as a libation upon the sacrificial offering of your faith" (Philippians 2:17). In the Book of Revelation, Saint John beheld the souls of the martyrs in heaven, and they were "under the altar" of sacrifice (Revelation 6:9).

In their suffering, the martyrs imitate Jesus in his martyrdom—in his witness. But they do more than that. Because of their communion, they participate in Jesus' once-for-all sacrifice. With Jesus, Christians share one common life: "I have been crucified with Christ; it is no longer I who live, but Christ who lives in me" (Galatians 2:20). As they have lived with Christ, so they die with him: "But if we have died with Christ, we believe that we shall also live with him" (Romans 6:8).

Communion with Christ is not a protection from suffering. It is a blessing of our suffering. It makes suffering not a curse, but an entryway to eternal life. Saint Paul proclaimed that we are "heirs of God and fellow heirs with Christ, provided we suffer with him in order that we may also be glorified with him" (Romans 8:17).

For the early Christians, the terms could not be made any clearer. When they spoke of their own impending martyrdom, they described it in Eucharistic terms. Saint Ignatius of Antioch, writing around 107, foresaw his death in the Roman Colosseum as a Mass. "I am the wheat of God," he wrote to the Church of Rome, "and let me be ground by the teeth of the wild beasts, that I may be found the pure bread of Christ."[1] He predicted that he would, like wine, "be poured out to God while the altar is still ready."[2] The Christians who attended his execution would be like the choir at Sunday Mass: "gathered together in love, you may sing praise to the Father, through Christ Jesus."[3] He invoked his priestly status as bishop and even quoted the Eucharistic prophecy of Malachi 1:11, noting that as a Syrian traveling to Rome he was moving from the rising of the sun to its setting.

To prepare for his final liturgy, Ignatius knew no better preparation than the Church's liturgy.

---

[1] Saint Ignatius of Antioch, *Letter to the Romans* 4.
[2] Ibid. 2.
[3] Ibid.

I have no delight in corruptible food, nor in the pleasures of this life. I desire the bread of God, the heavenly bread, the bread of life, which is the flesh of Jesus Christ, the Son of God, who became afterwards of the seed of David and Abraham; and I desire the drink of God, namely his blood, which is incorruptible love and eternal life.[4]

In the middle of the third century, Saint Cyprian prescribed daily Mass as the best preparation for courage in martyrdom. To the people of the town of Thibaris, he wrote: "The soldiers of Christ must equip themselves with weapons of unblemished faith and valorous strength, reflecting that the reason why they drink each day the cup of the blood of Christ is that they themselves may thus also be enabled to shed their blood for Christ's sake."[5]

Cyprian spoke of the Eucharist as the Christian's spiritual armor and weaponry—the Church's only hope as it faced mortal combat with demonic powers.

And, as the Eucharist is appointed for this very purpose that it may be a safeguard to the receivers, it is needful that we may arm those whom we wish to be safe against the adversary with the protection of the Lord's abundance. For how do we teach or provoke them to shed their blood in confession of his name if

---

[4] Ibid. 7.
[5] Saint Cyprian of Carthage, *Letters* 58.1.2.

we deny to those who are about to enter on the warfare the blood of Christ? Or how do we make them fit for the cup of martyrdom, if we do not first admit them to drink, in the Church, the cup of the Lord by the right of communion?[6]

This passage explains why persecuted Christians, down through the ages, have been willing to take grave risks in order to celebrate the Mass. In Elizabethan England, Catholic aristocrats outfitted their mansions with "priest holes" for hiding. In communist prison camps, the Faithful gathered in the shelter of outspread newspapers. During the Diocletian persecution, the people exposed themselves simply by meeting on Sunday, which was an ordinary workday. They told their judge: "We cannot live without the Mass."[7]

United with Christ in Holy Communion, the martyrs faced death not with their own weakness, but with Jesus' strength. Saint Perpetua of Carthage gave birth while she was in prison, and her jailers mocked her as she cried out in labor. They said her sufferings in the arena would be much worse. But she replied: "Now it is I who suffer what I am suffering; then, there will be another in me who will suffer for me, because I will be suffering for him."[8] So close is the communion between the Christian and Christ, that they share a common life, a common struggle, a common death, and a common glory.

---

[6] Ibid., 3.2 (To Cornelius, "Concerning Granting Peace to the Lapsed").

[7] *Acts of the Martyrs of Abitina.*

[8] *The Passion of the Holy Martyrs Perpetua and Felicity* 5.2.

I am not the first to notice this Eucharistic motif in the lives and testimonies of the martyrs.[9] Pope Benedict XVI took a special interest in it, and he made it a key point in his great letter on the Eucharist, *Sacramentum Caritatis*.

> The Christian who offers his life in martyrdom enters into full communion with the Pasch of Jesus Christ and thus becomes Eucharist with him. Today too, the Church does not lack martyrs who offer the supreme witness to God's love. Even if the test of martyrdom is not asked of us, we know that worship pleasing to God demands that we should be inwardly prepared for it. Such worship culminates in the joyful and convincing testimony of a consistent Christian life, wherever the Lord calls us to be his witnesses.[10]

Pope Benedict made clear that this is not a matter of purely academic interest. It is relevant to our daily lives. Very few of us will be called to martyrdom of blood, but we are all called to witness "wherever the Lord calls us."

As we live the liturgy within the Church, we cannot help but prepare for this task. We hear the Word of God in the

---

[9] It is developed, for example, in many works of contemporary scholars. See Cardinal Joseph Ratzinger, *Pilgrim Fellowship of Faith: The Church as Communion* (San Francisco: Ignatius, 2005), 112–114; Robin Darling Young, *In Procession Before the World: Martyrdom as Public Liturgy in Early Christianity* (Milwaukee: Marquette University Press, 2001); Scott Hahn, *Letter and Spirit: From Written Text to Living Word in the Liturgy* (New York: Image, 2005), 102–106; and Mike Aquilina, *Ministers and Martyrs* (Manchester, NH: 2015), 79–86.

[10] Pope Benedict XVI, Post-Synodal Apostolic Exhortation *Sacramentum Caritatis*, n. 85; see also n. 72.

readings. In the homily we are exhorted to apply it to our lives. In the offertory we place our lives with the gifts on the altar—we "let go and let God." In the Eucharistic Prayer we make the offering with Jesus. And in communion we receive his life in exchange for our own.

We make a habit, then, of our self-offering, just as Ignatius did, and Perpetua, and Cyprian—and just as those great martyrs instructed us to do.

Our entire life is a participation in the liturgy established by Jesus Christ and entrusted to the Church. Our entire life is offered in the Mass, and through the Mass we come to share the life and identity of Jesus. As the New Testament tells us, we become "partakers of the divine nature" (2 Peter 1:4).

We are all going to die. (That should arrive as news to no one.) How blessed is death for those who die in communion with Christ—no matter the circumstances of their death. How much more blessed are the martyrs; for they die a death that is the likeness of Jesus' own. They die a death that is Eucharistic, life-giving, offered freely for the sake of others.

CHAPTER 13
The Ecumenism of Blood

Many people today—and terrorist cells, and even nations—declare themselves to be enemies of Jesus Christ, his Church, and his cause. They persecute the Church, and they make martyrs, because they think this will weaken Christ.

They are wrong. History demonstrates that the Church grows stronger, more numerous, and more united from the blood shed by martyrs.

I believe that, in our time, *unity* is a particular gift the martyrs are bestowing on the greater Church. What we Christians have failed to achieve through interchurch dialogue, God is achieving through grace as persecuted Christians come to share a common underground.

Pope Francis calls this "the ecumenism of blood." In a 2013 interview with Italian journalist Andrea Tornielli, he explained what he meant by that phrase:

> Today there is an ecumenism of blood. In some countries they kill Christians for wearing a cross or having a Bible and before they kill them they do not ask them whether they are Anglican, Lutheran, Catholic or Orthodox. Their blood is mixed. To those who kill we

are Christians. We are united in blood, even though we have not yet managed to take necessary steps towards unity between us and perhaps the time has not yet come. Unity is a gift that we need to ask for.

I knew a parish priest in Hamburg who was dealing with the beatification cause of a Catholic priest guillotined by the Nazis for teaching children the catechism. After him, in the list of condemned individuals, was a Lutheran pastor who was killed for the same reason. Their blood was mixed. . . . Those who kill Christians don't ask for your identity card to see which Church you were baptized in.[1]

In the months that followed that interview, we saw the principle in action again and again in the murders perpetrated by members of the Islamic State and Boko Haram. In 2015 Pope Francis told Coptic Pope Tawadros II that an "ecumenism of blood unites us."

The phrase appears frequently in the Holy Father's homilies, addresses, letters, and video messages. The cause of the martyrs is clearly and constantly on his heart. "The blood of our Christian brothers and sisters is a testimony which cries out to be heard. It makes no difference whether they be Catholics, Orthodox, Copts, or Protestants. They are Christians! Their blood is one and the same. Their blood confesses Christ."[2]

[1] Andrea Tornielli, "Never Be Afraid of Tenderness," *La Stampa* (December 14, 2013): archived at lastampa.it.

[2] Pope Francis, Address to the Moderator and Representatives of the Church of Scotland, February 16, 2015.

This is powerful rhetoric, but it reflects a more powerful reality.

There is abundant testimony from the communist and Nazi eras of Christians working together, underground, in spite of their denominational differences.

In the Middle East there have been very practical ecumenical breakthroughs. In the last three decades, Chaldean Catholics have breached a divide with the Assyrian Church of the East that dates back to the fifth century. As these believers witnessed to their common devotion to Jesus, they recognized that their faith was the same. In 1994 the Assyrian Patriarch Mar Dinkha IV joined with Pope Saint John Paul II to sign a "Common Christological Declaration." In 2001, the Pontifical Council for Promoting Christian Unity (which I now have the privilege of serving as a member) approved the sharing of Communion between the (Catholic) Chaldean Church and the Assyrian Church of the East.

I myself have seen—and participated in—these breakthroughs. In September 2014 my city was host to a "summit" meeting of patriarchs from the Middle East. Attending were five patriarchs from the Middle East, as well as representatives from other patriarchates: Maronite Patriarch Mar Bechara Boutros Cardinal Raï; Melkite Greek Catholic Patriarch Gregorius III Laham; Syriac Orthodox Patriarch Mor Ignatius Aphrem II; Syriac Catholic Patriarch Ignatius Youssef III Yonan; Armenian Apostolic Catholicos Aram I Keshishia; Orthodox Christian Metropolitan Joseph Al-Zehlaoui; Coptic Orthodox Bishop Angaelos; and Chaldean Bishop-emeritus

Ibrahim. They met to discuss—and begin to develop—a common, comprehensive strategy to overcome extremism that threatens the very survival of Christianity in places like Iraq and Syria.

Humiliated alike and driven to the same catacombs, Christians may at last come to put aside old resentments and see our differences with greater clarity and charity—and resolve them, for the sake of survival. From the martyrs we may learn to put aside pride, centuries-old resentment, and personal prejudice and encounter one another in truth.

And even when we cannot share communion, we can stand together, pray together, support one another, and defend one another's rights, reputation, property—and lives.

⚜

"You will be my witnesses," said Jesus. "You will be my *martyrs* . . . to the ends of the Earth" (Acts 1:8).

Thus he gave us, along with his privileges and promises, full disclosure of the cost of discipleship. The Apostles understood. Saint Peter told the first Christians that they should consider themselves "aliens and exiles" in this world (1 Peter 2:11). "Here," we read in the Letter to the Hebrews, "we have no lasting city" (13:14).

So, as strangers and foreigners, we will go through life. And we will be misunderstood and distrusted.

We should not be surprised, then, when people treat

us as interlopers and a threat—even as we are loving them unconditionally.

We should not be surprised when people today, like Nero long ago, accuse us of "hatred of humanity"—when they call us bigots and charge us with discrimination for daring to speak the truth in love.

We should not be surprised when, like the Emperor Julian, rulers try to legally exclude us from the professions and from participation in civic life.

We should not be surprised when, like King Henry, they say we are disloyal citizens who follow a foreign king.

We want to stand with our King, Jesus, and live with him—and, like the martyrs, die with him, if that is the will of God.

If you and I should be called to such witness, we should remember that we do not stand alone. We stand with the whole Church on earth. We stand with the saints and angels.

In the meantime, we must make it our mission to stand with those who *are* suffering today. We must stand in solidarity with them and re-echo their testimony to all the world.

Postscript

On August 6, 2015, Pope Francis addressed the following letter to the Auxiliary Bishop of Jerusalem and Patriarchal Vicar in Jordan, Maroun Lahham.

Dear Brother,

I take advantage of the visit to Jordan of His Excellency Archbishop Nunzio Galantino, Secretary General of the Italian Bishops' Conference, to reach with a word of hope so many people who oppressed by violence, have been forced to abandon their homes and their land.

Time and time again I have wished to give voice to the atrocious, inhuman and inexplicable persecutions of those, who in many parts of the world—and especially amongst Christians—are victims of fanaticism and intolerance, often under the eyes and in the silence of all. They are the martyrs of today, humiliated and discriminated against for their faith in the Gospel.

My words, which appeal for solidarity, are the sign of a Church that does not forget and that does not abandon her children who have been exiled on account of their faith: they must know that a daily prayer is raised for them, and that we are grateful for the witness they offer.

My thoughts also go to the Communities that have not

looked away and are taking care of these brothers of ours. You proclaim the resurrection of Christ by sharing the pain and by giving help to hundreds of thousands of refugees. Bowing before the misery that risks stifling their hope, your fraternal service illuminates the dark moments of their existence.

May the Lord reward you as only he can, with an abundance of gifts.

And may world opinion be more attentive, sensitive and sympathetic before the persecutions carried out against Christians, and in general, against religious minorities.

I renew my hope that the international community will not assist in silence without taking action in the face of this unacceptable crime, a crime that constitutes an alarming drift from the most basic of human rights which prevents a rich cohabitation between peoples, cultures and faiths.

Please, I ask you to pray for me.

May the Lord bless you and Our Lady protect you.

—FRANCISCUS

Works Consulted

John L. Allen, Jr., *The Global War on Christians: Dispatches from the Front Lines of Anti-Christian Persecution* (New York: Image, 2013).

Mike Aquilina, *Ministers and Martyrs* (Manchester, NH: Sophia Institute Press, 2015).

———— *The Witness of Early Christian Women: Mothers of the Church* (Huntington, IN: Our Sunday Visitor, 2014).

Rod Bennett, *Four Witnesses: The Early Church in Her Own Words* (San Francisco: Ignatius Press, 2002).

G.W. Bowersock, *Martyrdom and Rome* (Cambridge, UK: Cambridge University Press, 2002).

Elizabeth Castelli, *Martyrdom and Memory: Early Christian Culture Making* (New York: Columbia University Press, 2004).

Walter Ciszek, *He Leadeth Me* (San Francisco: Ignatius Press, 1993).

———— *With God in Russia* (San Francisco: Ignatius Press, 1997).

Rory T. Conley, *Witnesses to Jesus Christ: A History of the Catholic Church in the First Millennium* (Washington, DC: CreateSpace, 2014).

Robert J. Daly, S.J., *Christian Sacrifice* (Washington, DC: Catholic University of America Press, 1978).

Eamon Duffy, *The Stripping of the Altars: Traditional Religion in England 1400–1580* (New Haven, CT: Yale, 1992).

Gerolamo Fazzini, *The Red Book of Chinese Martyrs* (San Francisco: Ignatius Press, 2009).

George Heyman, *The Power of Sacrifice: Roman and Christian Discourses in Conflict* (Washington, DC: Catholic University of America Press, 2007).

Svitlana Hurkina and Rev. Andriy Mykhaleyko, eds., *To the Light of Resurrection through the Thorns of Catacombs: The Underground Activity and Reemergence of the Ukrainian Greek Catholic Church* (L'viv: Ukrainian Catholic University Press, 2014).

Philip Jenkins, *The New Anti-Catholicism: The Last Acceptable Prejudice* (New York: Oxford University Press, 2003).

Theresa Marie Moreau, *Blood of the Martyrs: Trappist Monks in Communist China* (Los Angeles, CA: Veritas Est Libertas, 2013).

Herbert Musurillo, ed. and trans. *The Acts of the Christian Martyrs* (Oxford: Oxford University Press, 1972).

Terrye Newkirk, OCDS, *The Mantle of Elijah: The Martyrs of Compiègne as Prophets of the Modern Age* (Washington, DC: Institute of Carmelite Studies, 1995).

Jaroslav Pelikan, *Brazos Theological Commentary Bible: Acts* (Grand Rapids, MI: Brazos, 2005).

Giuseppe Ricciotti, *The Age of Martyrs: Christianity from Diocletian to Constantine.* (Milwaukee: Bruce, 1959).

Robert Royal, *The Catholic Martyrs of the Twentieth Century: A Comprehensive World History* (New York: Crossroad, 2000).

J.J. Scarisbrick, *Henry VIII* (Berkeley: University of California Press, 1968).

Marta Sordi, *The Christians and the Roman Empire* (Norman, OK: University of Oklahoma Press), 1994.

Robin Darling Young, *In Procession Before the World: Martyrdom as Public Liturgy in Early Christianity* (Milwaukee: Marquette University Press, 2001).

Rodney Stark, *The Rise of Christianity: How the Obscure, Marginal Jesus Movement Became the Dominant Re-*

ligious Force in the Western World in a Few Centuries (San Francisco: HarperCollins, 1997).

—— *Cities of God: The Real Story of How Christianity Became an Urban Movement and Conquered Rome* (San Francisco: Harper, 2006).

D. Vincent Twomey and Mark Humphries, eds., *The Great Persecution: The Proceedings of the Fifth Patristic Conference, Maynooth, 2003* (Dublin: Four Courts, 2009).

Robert Louis Wilken, *The First Thousand Years: A Global History of Christianity* (New Haven, CT: Yale University Press 2013).

Donald W. Wuerl, *The Forty Martyrs: New Saints of England and Wales* (Huntington, IN: Our Sunday Visitor, 1971).

Bat Ye'or, *The Decline of Eastern Christianity under Islam: From Jihad to Dhimmitude* (Madison, NJ: Fairleigh Dickinson University Press, 1996).